Old Homes,
Old Places,
Old Memories

Linda Lee

FIRST EDITION,
Copyright © 2019 by Linda Lee
All Rights Reserved.

No portion of this book may be reproduced without permission of the author.

ISBN: 9781081442286

Dedication

I remember the moment they laid my first born in my arms and looking down, thinking she is part me, part him and your life changes, never the same again. The second one comes with curly red hair and you think you have cloned yourself. Your life is fuller and much busier and one comes along that must be buried, must go back to where they've come from and your heart breaks. You watch your two grow and wonder what could have been.

You get on with life, getting ahead, making plans, unaware how fast the years are passing. In the busyness of life your children have grown and the years that have passed so quickly for you are now just beginning for them. The magic day finally arrives and your first grandchild is laid in your arms. Of course you love your kids, but that grandchild is the new beginning, it's the child you always have time for, they are the teacher that shows you getting ahead is not so important, all the unimportant things you took so serious are not so important anymore.

All the hard work has paid off and you now have time for the magic of grandchildren. Your heart is not yours anymore, it belongs to them. I see one full of dreams, a builder of things, a writer, an artist, a movie maker, a catcher of dreams, another hard headed, also an artist, horse lover, country inside and out; another a beauty queen, hard headed, opinioned, beautiful and loving, another, half country, half town, a horse lover and a little hard headed too, also an artist and the last grandchild, a blonde cutie that stays in the background. She too is an artist, but like her oldest sister prefers not to roll around in the dirt or work up a sweat around barns and such. Each one is precious and a gift from God.

Ah but then the great grand kids start coming. By now your walk has really slowed and you find the table much easier to play on, the floor demands to much creaking of the knees to get down to set up soldiers. You delight in seeing the faces of grandkids when they hold their children. Only you know how fast the time will pass until the next generation comes along. The first born of my first born does not know the love that awaits him, growing inside his wife, part him, part her. This bundle will make 5 g.grands. I know I won't live long enough to see them become builders, writers, but perhaps I can see their dreams take form.

How I thank our Lord for the blessings he has given me. A wild teenager marries a hard working young man and our love has brought forth more blessings than I ever deserved and tonight I thank the Lord for his guidance, for my salvation and ask him to watch over my children and theirs, to protect the steps of the wee ones and guide all to his wonderful saving grace. Truly, I've been blessed. This book I dedicate to them.

Table of Contents

HOPE

The Latter Rain..2
Snow, Bluegrass and the Plaid Man...................4
Dresses and Violet Bouquets............................7
Take Me Back..9
Quilts of Life..10
Patti's Saddles...11
Vodka Jim..13
Two Dresses..15
At The Sound Of His Trump............................17
Wishin', Prayin' and Hopein'...........................18
A Day Written Down.......................................20
Bedside Thoughts 22
A Child's Perception.......................................24
Wishful Thinking...26
Once A Governor's Home...............................28
Perhaps The Whispering Breeze....................30
The Gulf Hammock Creek...............................32

HEARTACHE

The Klinton Hits...35.
Shamrock and Trolls.......................................37
Borders, Plows and Real Estate.....................39
A Graveyard of Vets..43
The Dying Garden...45

Table of Contents

A Moment In Time...47
For Now..49
Stuff...
Swamp Roach..52
THE BROWARD COWARD...............................54
Twas The Month Before Christmas.................56
The Phantom..58
The Spirits..60
The Storm...62
The Visitor..63
The Kill Pen..66
A Woman's Thoughts in '64.............................68
Beer Cans and Dead Dogs..............................71
Wild Moors and Willowed Glen......................72
The Unexpected Guest....................................74
The Voice and Time of Nature.........................76
On A Rainy Day..77
When The Welcome Sign Is Not Out..............78
Unspoken Words...82
When Once There Was A Lane.......................84
Who Is To Know?...86
Suffer the Little Children..................................88
The Ash Heap of History..................................90
When The Last One Has Left..........................91
Angry? Not Hardly..93
One Potato, Two Potato...................................95

Table of Contents

HOME

Two Ladies..97
Gone Is Forever..99
A Hundred Years Of Footsteps.....................101
Saying Good-bye To A Friend......................104
Brightly Boxed and Bowed..........................106
The Man In My Life......................................108
Two Sisters..110
Thoughts on Turning 70..............................112
The Spider Path..115
Childhood to Manhood................................117
The Final Trail...119
Cleaning Day At The Barn..........................120
A Gleaning of Memories.............................122
Unsaid Words To A Dead Mother................124
Dolls..126
Just a Wednesday Afternoon Thought........130.
The Pasture Shack.....................................131
The Barrel..133
A Sister's Thoughts...................................135
Looking Back...138
Our Hands...140
Fifty Four and Counting.............................141
POW, POW, POW......................................143

Table of Contents

He Is Only Lent..................................144
Wasted Time.....................................145
No Option..147
On A Visit To His Daughter's Home...................148
Perhaps a Memory................................149
The Porch Railing................................150
When You Called Me Lynn.........................151
The Flood..152
Sad Thoughts Nearing Christmas....................156
A Poem for My Sister.............................158
Sleepless in Florida...............................162

Acknowledgements................................16

The Latter Rain

I hear the sound of distant rain
Beginning to come near,
The promises of long ago
Are starting to appear.
Along the far horizon
I see the white attire,
My ears are picking up the sound
Of heaven's angel choir.
I've heard it sung he could have called
Ten thousand to his side,
But now he's getting ready for
His supper and his bride.
I hear the voice of God's own son,
He readies to step out
And soon the earth will tremble at
His long awaited shout.
And in a moment those that have
His precious blood upon
The hearts and souls that heard his word
In a moment shall be gone.
I sit and ponder old church house
And souls that have been saved,
The little children and the old
That wait there in the grave.
The rain is just beginning,
I hear and recognize
That soon those graves will open up

And his people start to rise.
This old church house has seen its day,
But rain will surely flood
And only those who will escape
Are those under his blood.
The day is short, the night is long
And I have little doubt,
The latter rain is falling
And we'll soon hear heaven's shout.

Snow, Bluegrass and the Plaid Man

Thoughts drifted with river currents,
Past festivals, beyond bluegrass music
And playing children.
He disturbed my pine needle braiding,
This stranger with a dialect from the north,
With plaid shorts, knee high stockings
And legs whiter than the snow he spoke of.
He talked of his hometown,
Unaware I hadn't asked the first question.
He conversed about snowplows and Pittsburgh,
Steel mills and smoke.
When I didn't respond, he asked,
"Where are you from?"

"Never been further north than the Carolinas
or west of Texas,
Never touched snow, had chains on my tires
Or had much yearning to leave the state."
I was satisfied that ended our conversation
But the plaid man continued.

"Don't have much bluegrass in Pittsburgh
And we call a fiddle, a violin."
He went on about so few homes along the river.
"I guess people don't make much money here," he said,
"Probably can't afford the land."

My pine needle braiding came to an abrupt halt.
I asked him to squint his eyes
And look across the river.
"See that glint in the sunset?
A marker for my great, great grandpa."
He cupped his hands around his eyes
Until he was sure he saw the sparkle.
"Can't build factories, houses and smokestacks
Over a history marker," I reminded.
Being the absolute correct time to continue my story
And mostly because he didn't ask
I told him about the man in my far away past.
"he was a blockade runner,
A man of sugar, whiskey and lace.
A man who knew these waters
and the secrecy of the forest beyond.
A man who never knew Pittsburgh,
Didn't touch snow and had no need for sleds.
A man who loved to play the fiddle."

Without waiting for me to continue
He left, blue socks and veined legs
disappearing near the food stands.
I wondered if he were eating
or talking of Pittsburgh.
I started braiding again, watching coots,
Thinking of my great, great grandpa,
Who never ran a blockade or played the fiddle,
Who never put his foot south of Georgia.

Later I saw the plaid man,
Heard him talking to a fiddle player
Who must not have known a story

And had no marker to point out.
I could have been polite,
Letting him talk
of weather and Pittsburgh,
But then he would have missed the granite marker
That only glinted in my mind.

Dresses and Violet Bouquets

I went through Granny's bureau
Just the other day
And there between the things she had
Were pressed violet bouquets.
Her clothes brought back the memories
As I sat upon her bed
And touched the bonnets that she wore,
Held Bible, worn and read.
She never had the fancy things,
Plain eyelet, never lace
And as I held a part of her
The tears streamed down my face.
But it was in her closet........
That I could not go through,
Her dresses hung upon the peg
And broke my heart in two.
Granny's life was one of work
But through it she was blest.
I reached and got one from the peg
And held it to my breast.
It's wiped away the teardrops
Of a tiny, little child,
Had pockets for the violets
That grew profuse and wild.
It often held the chicken eggs
From those escaping pen
And once I saw it wrapped around

A skinny, dying hen.
She often swished the flies away
As she sat shelling peas,
With just the hem of that old dress
She'd make a summer breeze.
I still can see them on the line
Drying in the sun,
But now the clotheslines worn thin
And is not used for one.
My granny has been carried home
By angels late last year,
But once again as I sat there
Her dress will dry a tear.
Her violets still push up through shade
Of honeysuckle vine.
I hold the dress and wish for years
They hung out on the line.
goes with dresses and violets

Take Me Back

I try to keep our past alive
And carry on the torch,
To days of slower livin'
When we all sat on the porch.
When A/C was a shady tree
And windows opened wide,
When 10' ceilings let in air
That cooled the whole inside.
When children played out in the yard
And dogs did not need fence,
When talk was plain and courteous
And no one took offense.
When people knew just who they were
And Sunday School was full,
When we were taught the Golden Rule
And all were merciful.
Take me back to tree lined lanes
And shady Sunday walks,
When women, kids and men converse,
No worries how one talks.
Take me back to Granny's life,
Times were quiet, slow
And let me sit upon a porch,
Built many years ago.

Quilts of Life

He holds my arm, so not to fall, I lean against his chest,
This house will be our resting place, both his and my request.
Today my quilts blow in the wind, the patterns of my life;
Memories of the day we came, he husband, me a wife.
We had a little, baby boy, I dressed him all in blue.
I did not know the years we shared would be so very few.
A tiny shirt, not yet wore out, within a piece of hair,
A piece of bonnet shaded him, now in this corner square.
The clothes we used to bury him, I cut a snippet out,
And now I fear no one will know what these are all about.
The rings were made of memories from years that went to fast;
The births and deaths of those I loved, the pieces of my past.
Now heaven's stars swing on my line, the closest to the door,
The one I hold so dear to me, the son that went to war.
I so remember darkened day when someone came to tell,
Our son would not be coming home, was hit with shot and shell.
This special one I hold to me, his life seemed such a theft,
I touch the ragged, worn squares, tis all that I have left.
This house is old, seen better days, no one comes around,
Chatter of my children are now birds that make the sound.
I hold his hand, we look about and ponder days gone by.
I'll fold my quilts, put them away and love them till I die.
He holds my arm, that I not slip, I grasp his aged hand
And hope someone will one day stop and they will understand
That tattered bits of memory are all that occupies
And hope that after we have gone, their story never dies.

Patti's Saddles

Tis the tale of the woe b'gone saddles,
dusty and long put aside,
One saddle held all the memories,
on a rack, displayed there with pride.
All looking for someone to use them,
to again feel a human's touch,
to warm the back of another horse,
replace billets and conchos and such.
But three saddles lay on a truck bed,
and I wondered what each of them knew,
while people looked at the new tack,
with three saddles just out of view.
How many kids pulled up cinches,
what was their heaviest load,
had the horses worked or just pleasured
and what was the prettiest road.
I thought of the horses that used them,
were they grade or some finely bred,
But I knew by the age of the saddles,
the horses, most likely, were dead.
Yet I know each saddle has memories,
for once each one had been new,
now their tossed in the bed of a pickup,
forgotten and just out of view.
But one saddle was out in the open,
placed there on a saddle rack,
calling to shoppers to come take a look

as it sat there amid other tack.
The seller told buyers the story,
of a son that now doesn't ride;
traded horses for hunting and fishing,
to busy with child and a bride.
In time a man bought the saddle,
she sold bridles and bits thru the day,
but her heart quivered ever so slightly
as she watched him haul saddle away.
For in years to come her son's saddle
would be sold to buy something new,
and like three saddles there in the truck bed-
forgotten and just out of view.
And it struck me how much of a lifetime
could be written in this silly yarn,
and how often we let go of memories,
to gain more space in the barn.

Vodka Jim

As I sit on my back porch rememberin'
Of days that have long since gone by,
Don't know where the time has all gone too,
Just know I ain't ready to die.
My eyes have seen all the changes,
My ears have heard all the sounds,
I've seen cars clog all the highways
And people clog all of the towns.
The bowlegs of mine were once strong,
My hands were once fists of steel,
My cowboy hat ain't changed much lately
An I still can get spurs on my heels.
Horses, I've trained em and tamed em,
Broke em an whipped em some too,
I've lived long and hard thru a lifetime
And done what I set out to do.
I've wrangled along with the best of the bunch,
Branded and roped many steers,
I've honkey tonked most of the night spots,
Done more than my share it appears.
Cause this vodka sure makes rememberin'
Grow sweeter an better with age.
Now my eyes see the old, long dead cowboys
On the magazine's ragged, worn page.
Why I could'a been one of them pictures,
Rough men ready to fight,
Never had no fancy learnin',

But sure knew what wrong was from right.
Memories don't mean much to no one
An life just goes speedin' on by,
Don't know where the time has all gone to,
But I'm makin' more for I die.
As I sit lookin' back at a lifetime,
I'm glad what I turned out to be,
The Lord didn't make me a rich man,
But my memories worth millions to me.

                                        2/16/74

Two Dresses

I went to the re-enactment, I knew I should not stop,
But sure enough I slowed down and entered sutler's shop.
I didn't need more dresses, that fact was absolute.
I had no need for bonnets, fans, no corset, button boot.
But I just could not pass it by, it wouldn't be polite,
Was then I saw the dresses there, one green, one ivory white.
I slipped one from the hanger, the satin swished and swooped,
It fell away in green cascades, or'e head and 'round my hoop.
I buttoned up the bodice, the dress had not one flaw,
I smiled into the mirror, surprised at what I saw.
The tent flap now was open, a door was thrown wide.
The coolness of the upper floor beckoned me outside.
The shaded gallery looked upon, oaks lining curvy drive.
I pinched myself to just make sure that I was still alive.
The fragrance of magnolias in early springtime bloom,
Filled the porch, the halls, the stair and scented every room.
Was then I heard my name called out, I hurried down the stair,
With button shoes, lacy fan and flowers in my hair.
I did not stop to think, recall, that I had not dressed so,
But opened wide the parlor doors and entered long ago.
Twin fiddles played a lonely waltz, with barely room to stand,
My green dress sparkled in the night, was then he touched my hand.
This man I did not know by name, like memories just displaced,
A familiar touch as he reached out, his hand about my waist.
I smiled, he laughed, we danced all night, my dress swirled 'cross the floor.

I tried to paint him in my mind, we must have met before.
The fiddles slowed and candlelight was growing very dim,
He bowed and touched my hand once more, I said good-by to him.

Was then I heard the cannons boom and time would not allow,
For outside lines were forming for the re-enactment now.
I held the other hanger with the dress so ivory white
And as I slipped it or'e my head, it glimmered in the light.
Again the tent held shadows from the candle's eerie glow
And as I buttoned bodice up, I stepped back long ago.

I could hear the hum of voices, I could hear the fiddle's bow,
Then soft piano started from the room there just below.
This time it was camellias, their blossoms all were planned,
To go with just the single rose that I held in my hand.
My eyes were growing misty in the wedding dress I wore,
He held my hand and vowed his love, familiar, as before.
He had a saber on his side, (I thought I shouldn't stay)
His boots were polished shiny black, his frock coat, pressed and gray.
I was not sure, but felt so safe, I feared he'd disappear,
I smiled and held familiar hand of one that stood so near.
The Reverend smiled and looked about, then offered up his prayers.
Though celebration did not stop, he led me up the stairs.
The modest curtain hid me well, the dress fell to the floor,
Suddenly all things have changed to what they were before.
The sutler's tent was dark and hot, the dresses were not there,
I had on jeans and cowboy boots, no flowers in my hair.
I stood there for a moment, not sure of where I'd been
And tried to pull up pictures of those two familiar men.
I heard my husband calling, the battle had begun,
Men stood in line and fired, was just smoke and sound of gun.
And for the next few moments, smoke covered sky and land,
My husband cupped his eyes to see and then I knew the hand.

At The Sound Of His Trump

"Is this the child?" the angel asked, "The one we're waiting for?
He looks no different than the rest that's birthed on earth before.
Is it his name that's written down, the last one in your book?"
Then as the child gained his breath the gates of heaven shook.
The cherubs and the cherubim's praised God with Holy joy
And angels knew the shout was near, this was the baby boy.
Years in heaven are but a day and the boy was swiftly grown,
A number in the universe, untried, untrue, unknown.
For drugs and whiskey did their trick, a wasted life it seemed,
But the Master of the universe knew he could be redeemed.
The King of Kings and Lord of Lords knew the man's despair,
Around the throne both day and night were words of mother's prayer.

Late one night the thunder roared and the gates of heaven shook,
A checkmark had been placed upon a name in heaven's book.
A man was on his knees that night, tears glistened on his face,
Whiskey, drugs, the filth of sin now covered by God's grace.
"Is this the child?" the angel asked, "The one your waiting for,
He looks so different than the rest that's birthed on earth before."
Ten thousands and ten thousands came into heavenly view,
While here on earth time had stopped and heavens trumpet blew.

Wishin', Prayin' and Hopein'

Blood drips, salted and torn to pieces
From inside a brightly lit room,
D.C. ordained the female is boss
And can now kill the life in her womb.
People marched, they held rallies and protests,
Met with signs for their street rendezvous,
They hope that the feds would all change their mind
And watched as the body parts grew.
The Christians sang songs at their service,
An elder would stand up to pray,
While a baby is scooped into black plastic bag
And casually thrown away.
God can't be mentioned to children,
An edict comes down from D.C,
Always stay left and never offend
And the gov't all seems to agree.
The Christians then come to their meetings
And an elder stands up to pray,
All the while gov't schools seem to grow
And the problem does not go away.
Drugs and sex are sold on the corner,
At the movies, TV and the store,
Yet most seem content to sit by the side
And wish things were as before.
The music is rap, theft and murder,
Clothes bare the breast and the crack,
A war on drugs and on terror?

But it's God that is under attack.
Once more, mostly Christians are silent,
From their churches, some kneel and some pray,
No action is taken to rally the troops,
They just hope the sin goes away.

A Day Written Down

On this shaded porch, the ceiling fan
Whirs softly down upon the slat swing.
Bees flirt and touch the jasmine
That twines around the pillars of my memory.
Most others are asleep or resting,
But my restless spirit pushes the swing
While I stare down the lane
And watch for his coming.
Today he will be here, Miss Winnie said so.
I see a visitor, but he is not my grandson,
He carries no book.
Miss Winnie said he called yesterday,
Or was it the day before?
I must remember this day,
Perhaps Miss Winnie might write it down.
My grandson will come with a tablet,
Most writers do, you know.
Then Miss Winnie can read me his words...
Over and over.

His eyes are mine now,
He sees things I could never imagine.
He is coming to read me his book,
On this porch, today or tomorrow.
I remember him pushing a porch swing
On the unclouded days of my memory,
His eyes wide in disbelief

Over such things as dragons and maidens.
On yesterday's porch we snuggled
While hand held fans cooled the afternoons
Of panther hunts and Indian attacks.
Together we conquered all evil,
Not willing to leave one dragon not slain.
While I wait to hear new tales,
I'll listen to the bees and smell the jasmine
And rock away years,
Remembering chubby hands clicking pretend guns
Down rimmed canyons.
Miss Winnie said my grandson was coming.
He will read and we will remember our yesterdays…
Today or tomorrow.

Bedside Thoughts

I think that most things in this life
Are good, yet some offend,
And through the decades there will be,
Beginnings and an end.
I often think of all the firsts
And all the years that passed,
And last night wondered 'bout the name
That will be written last.
What name through all the ages,
Within and all through out
Will be the last one written down
Before we hear his shout.
Is God's almighty angel
Beginning to rejoice,
And heaven's waiting patiently
For us to hear his voice?
The trump of God is ready now,
The worldly earth athirst,
While million eyes have shunned the truth,
The dead in Christ rise first.
Then we which are alive, remain,
Covered by blood's shroud,
We'll be there all together,
What a meeting in the cloud!
There will surely be rejoicing
At that meeting in the sky,
When death meets life that moment,

In the twinkling of an eye.
For narrow is the road to life,
Though love is open wide,
And oh what glory there will be
When Christ comes for his bride!
So many years ago was placed
Thorns for his crown
And now I wonder at the name,
The last one written down.
For through the years of all our lives
And through the centuries past,
I wonder at The Book Of Life
And who's name shall be last.

A Child's Perception

He was the lawgiver,
White haired and stern faced,
Full of "No's to a child
That held the devil in each hand.
On birthdays and holidays
He seemed friendlier,
But it was others who offered their laps,
Others who cajoled and laughed
At a child's antics.
He was a timeless river,
Never aging more than my first memory,
But always the lawgiver,
Hearing unsaid words, watching spilled milk,
Keeping track of lies.
I talked to him often,
Full of excuses over a days play.
He was always there,
Through Santa Clause and swings,
Listening as I moved unto movies, kisses
 And things that made him prick at my heart.
There were times we never spoke,
Though I knew he leaned forward,
Not wanting to miss a soft word,
Searching my face for a tear drop
That he could wipe away.
He was there to bless my first born
And touch my husband

Without ever letting me know.
Twenty-one years it took,
To understand this lawgiver, this trader
That swapped sin for life,
Who waited patiently
Until I put away my broomstick horse
And lingered while my swing rotted
And rusty roller skates were lost.
It was the lawgiver,
Who cooled the breeze in the country church
And pricked at my heart
And held me close when the tears finally came.
He was no longer the lawgiver,
But my Savior.

Wishful Thinking

Well over twenty years ago
I came across a buy
And bought the guitar on the spot
Before I wondered why.
My fingers could not strum the chords,
My ear for music's dead,
With loving hands I placed my buy
Beneath the double bed.
On occasion it came out,
It's strings were old with rust,
Thinking I could learn to play
I wiped away the dust.
Fingers never hit the string
That I was aiming for,
I slid the guitar back again
Along the dusty floor.
Two weeks ago I found a buy,
A banjo, less one string.
I hurried home with case in hand,
Then tried to play the thing.
For seven days I plunked and clanked,
Not once was ever bored,
I bought new picks and five new strings
But never made a chord.
Then in disgust I packed it up
And put it all away,
Insisting I would take the time

To learn to play one day.
I passed a store front yesterday,
The window in the middle,
With price marked down, displayed a case
With shabby bow and fiddle.
I checked my Visa, it was good,
"I'll be right back," I said,
But first I must go home and check
For space beneath my bed.

Once A Governor's Home, Live Oak, Florida
Cary A. Hardee (Florida Governor 1921-1925)

Who can say when it's to big,
When business clutters close,
They've torn it down and killed our past
And left us something gross.
A governor had picked this spot
In nineteen and o' four,
Chose the windows, picked the trim
And hung the heavy door.
He sat upon the shaded porch
And rocked through southern heat,
While many stopped and said hello
Out front, along the street.
But through the years the clutter came,
Progress is what they said
And no one cared to think about
What progress lay ahead.
Perhaps they never stopped to ask
Opinions of town folk.
Just decided bring it down,
A piece of old Live Oak.
And so began the tearing down,
The porch, the beams, the bricks
And it became a memory
In nineteen sixty-six.
There are no ghosts to settle in,
To wander in and out,

No pleasantness of long ago,
No past one cared about.
They covered lawn with hot asphalt,
Put signs to help promote,
A place for fries and burgers,
A place for root beer floats.
Exhaust has claimed the old oak trees
That shaded porch and hall
And one more piece of all our past
Is lost to ugly sprawl.
Tis sad for us when beauty leaves,
We've nothing from before
And in it's stead is southern sprawl
And ugly evermore.

Perhaps The Whispering Breeze

I thought I heard a whisper,
From the shadows deep within,
Perhaps it was the rustling leaves
That brushed the aging tin.
I thought I saw a shadow
As I stood there in the grass,
Perhaps it was reflections
In the old and wavy glass.
The path that once led to the door,
Was overgrown with need
For those to come and cut away
The briar and bramble weed.
But time is the eternal tick
For all the pioneers,
Time adds its burden to this home
That fights against the years.
Perhaps it was the summer breeze,
That blew around this place,
That whispered softly in my ear
And touched my arm and face.
Who will listen to the past,
Where homes once sat upon
And who shall write of long before
When old homes are all gone?

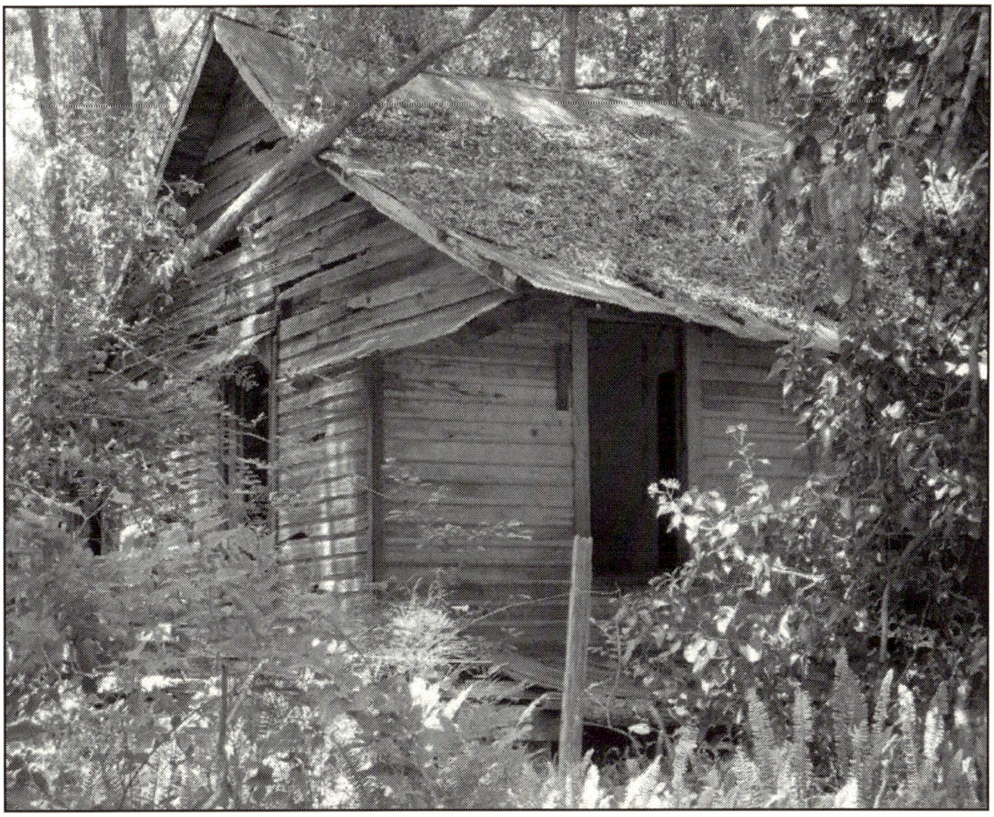

The Gulf Hammock Creek

The creek meanders through the trees
And knows the secrets well,
Its seen the saintly child of God,
Those on the path to hell.
The leaves have swept through open doors
That never more will close
And as the creek meanders by,
It talks 'bout all of those
Who sang the hymns of those long past,
Who came to reconcile,
Who gave their burdens to the Lord
And stepped out in the aisle.
Before the floor was warped and thin,
When inside was still dry,
Before piano played the hymns,
The creek meandered by.
The creek has swelled from many storms
And listened to wind blow,
The hammock lives on patiently,
While others come and go.
Birds nest among the rafters
That span high above the floor,
While critters of the hammock
Just walk in through open door.
Now walls have seen the changes there,
Once strong and now so frail
And still the creek meanders past

And knows 'bout every tale.
Once school was taught within these walls,
Now still, as if almost,
The chalkboard lingers on the floor,
For long awaited ghosts.
The air is musty from the heat,
In winter there's a chill,
The old church fights to keep its hold
And the creek meanders still.

Heartache

Photo by Andrea Sadock

The Klinton Hits

Charred bodies and the blackened bits,
Of women, children, Klinton hits;
Smoldering in the Texas sun
While snipers hide and fire guns.
What mother held her dying child
And gasped for air as flames went wild
And blackened all the Texas sky
While choppers, dozers, troops stood by.
Twisted arm will never hold
A crying baby, yet we're told,
They made their choice, stayed within
And Reno is the heroine.
They say it was the devil's nest
And only Reno knew what's best.
She sent her killers, sent their gear
And told us all, The buck stops here."
But who shall cry o'er infants grave,
To teach the truth in what they gave?
What smoke filled lungs cried unto God,
While Reno watched, how very odd
That flames and bullets all deprived
The life of those that stayed inside,
To fight against the tyranny
While TV cameras let us see
The smoking hulks of Klinton hits
That gave not one the benefit
Of freedom, for their guns would aim

At hearts and heads, none would remain,
To tell the tales of Klinton's sin;
To take them out, keep them within
The fiery walls that Reno lit
That covers up the Klinton hit.
I wonder if at night he hears,
A child's scream, a mother's tears?
But Reno tells us they had guns
And fire power by the tons.
Yet, who's to grieve that little heart
That Janet Reno blew apart?
I know it was her way to say,
Your guns will all be ours one day.
And while the ghosts of babies choke,
We'll hunker down and watch for smoke.
For Idaho and Waco sin
Has taught us all, we must begin
To clean our guns and save our lead;
Remember Waco, count the dead.
For it could well be you or I
That Janet Reno thinks should die.

1997

Shamrock and Trolls

I heard the rattling of his pots and pans,
His wagon creaked the streets about daylight,
But then I did not know his nightly plans
And no one cared about the old man's plight.
He once was rich with pillars washed in white
And owned the land that led down to the shore,
But that was years ago and long before
Her death had made his life a stumbling block.
She has been dead for years, at least three score,
But yet he smiles and talks to his 'Shamrock.'

He once had brought her hair pins and lace fans,
Would bow and kiss her hand to be polite,
I wonder at the years that he now spans
And strain to hear the words he will recite.
Perhaps within his prayers they reunite.
His wagon clinks and clatters to my door,
He asks for but a moment, nothing more
To sell a copper pan, a broken crock.
He writes the bill of sale, puts '94,
Still smiling as he talks to his 'Shamrock'.

He gathers up Sweet William and Queen Anne's,
To plant among the clover at her site,
She loved the heather of her Irish clans
and willowed glades where he could be her knight.,
The moon was full and gladly gave it's light

To churchyard gate and piney forest floor.
I've heard the stories told in Irish lore,
Of fairies dancing in the holly hock,
Now trolls have come and nightly they explore,
But yet he smiles and talks to his 'Shamrock'.

He bows his head and curses at the war,
With failing eyes now closed he hears no roar.
He's found the key to open up the lock
And death gave him what man could not restore.
He's kissed and touched the face of his 'Shamrock'.

Borders, Plows and Real Estate

The lane was long and dusty,
Eaten away from years of use,
Forgotten and tangled,
Unfit for the Model A
That bounced along it's ruts.
I had been there once,
To handle the estate,
To sell used up land
of memories and sharecroppers.
Maude was there then,
With red bandana and mens brogans,
She was there, bent like the oak limbs
That swooped close to the earth
And hindered my coming.

Maude and mule were in the field
Both walking rows
Each knew by heart.
She stopped and wiped her brow
With a hem that held
The dirt of many furrows.
"Dey say you be comin', she said
And for an instance a cloudy remembrance
Slipped past me and was swallowed up
Like hazy heat lines in the dust.

Hinges had rusted years ago
And chickens scratched around the open door,
Pecking at unseen things
In a yard swept clean
Of hoof prints and droppings.
It was peopled with memories,
This shack that did not burn.

How strange, I thought, to look upon
Ancestors protected by gilt frames,
Above newly limed floors.
"Dat's all dats lef," Maude said,
"pictures and dey's"
She handed me a ring,
Twelve polished keys that kept boundaries locked,

When bloodhounds trailed
Those that stepped over.

Maude's veined hands
Now carefully wrap
Ancestral pictures,
Packed in newspapers
She could not read.
The sing-song of island dialect
Told the journey of cotton fields and key-
holes,
Of suckled children long since dead
And hope where no hope had been.
I left her as I came,
Plowing rows where rows
Had been for a hundred years.
Keys, polished as a child,
Stayed behind, keeping her linked
To her past and her people.

Now I come again
With the sign never posted,
For Maude's harvests are over.
The fields have grown tall with fennel
And trough water, green and almost empty
Now buzz with mosquitoes.
A few chickens pecked the unraked dirt
From around the shack.
The chimneys left by the fire
Seemed like guard towers,
Castle walls crumbling
Where ivy has split the brick.
I could hear Maude's words,
"Dey say you be comin'."

The walls were yellowed,
Only where portraits had hung
Were they white.
There in a corner, balanced on two chairs,
Lay a door,
Rotten and rat gnawed,
A crocheted table cover folded in the center
And atop that, the keys,
Each dust free and polished.
From outside the chickens watched,
Stopped by an imaginary boundary,
As if Maude had swept them out
And locked the door behind her.

A Graveyard of Vets

They think because I'm dead
I can not hear,
Yet all these years
I've heard them come and go;
The rakes that sweep the autumn leaves away,
Their shovel digging holes for the new trees,
The mowers that cut grass and bump my stone.
I guess I should be glad they brought me home,
For german soil is not my resting place.
I was so young and how I had believed
That war was keeping liberty alive.
But in the family graveyard where I lay,
The preacher pounds his fist against the sin
And speaks of things I never thought I'd hear.
The iron rail and gates don't hold their words,
Just their way to separate me from them.

A year ago I heard the preacher say,
A man got by with killing wife and friend,
A week before they prayed for someone's son
Who shot some kids as they went out to play.
I hear them say that God is not a part
Of any school prayer that kids can say.
I thought I fought to stop this years ago.

Before the dew has dried upon the grass,
I hear the people rushing to their cars,

All anxious to get on with daily chores.
When I was put into this measured plot
The church was full and how I loved to hear
The preaching and the singing that was there.
Their voices are now scattered like the leaves.

Seems mostly now I hear the women's voice
And wonder where it is the men have gone.
I hear a prayer for babies never born,
Seems millions of them never took a breath.
My bones grow cold at Washington affairs
And I think of german soil I fought upon.

On Saturday the mowers will be here
And curses that would never leave my mouth
Will mingle with the clatter of the rakes.
Our tiny flags are bleached here in the sun,
Forgotten men that gave them liberty

The Dying Garden

Dogwoods first pushed forth their bloom,
Magnolias blossomed white,
Jasmine scented room by room,
Moon flowers scented night.
He pushed aside the words I said
And promised me a marriage bed.
I watched him dress and wondered why
A man can hardly wait to go,
So easily he said good by
And where he went I do not know.
Though blossoms fade and reappear
The roses did not bloom that year.

I wonder if a bud bursts forth
In tiny rose bouquet,
When winds blow from the chilly north
And a baby's on the way?
I hear the lonesome whippoorwill
And pray for spring and daffodil.

I fear my garden will not bloom
For all my days are gray.
I fashioned rock into a tomb
There in the garden, on display.
His baby neither breathed nor cried,
Along with him my garden died.
The old rock wall begins to crack,

There's not a flower I could save.
The trellis rose that grew out back
Are now dead flowers for a grave.
The willows weep but shed no tear,
They listen for the footsteps here.

The autumn wind has burned my face,
The leaves curl up and rot,
Death and dying fill this place
In spaces I've forgot.
I can't recall the roses smell…
Or when it was he bade farewell.

A Moment In Time

I walked among the many tombs and touched the smooth, gray stone.
I shut out all the voices 'round, till I was there alone.
I looked across the open fields, past decades all times ten,
I stared across the greening grass till I could hear the men.
I saw the cattle stand and stare at all the noise, debris,
Then one by one each cow and calf took refuge in the trees.
The shots at first were very dim, just echoes from the past,
But as I studied yonder ground, I heard the cannon blast.
So many men, I'd never seen a line that was that long,
Soldiers, horses, mules and boys, proud and marching strong.
To soon the lines were split apart and men began to fall,
I heard the grapeshot whistle past, the angry cannon ball.
I saw the gut shot horses, I heard their neighs and screams.
I saw the mules in bloody heaps, no longer now in teams.
The anguish that my eyes beheld was numbing, so profound,
As were the cries of fallen men, heaped there upon the ground.
There were no scattered men in death, piled corpses all about,
While hell delivered shot and shell, within and all thru out.
The smoke began to burn my eyes, heard splatters, pops and cracks,
Saw frenzied horses gallop past, no rider on their backs.
The battle raged for hours, though mere moments must have passed.
I looked again upon the fields, blood covered now by grass.

The screams and cries have faded, there's no soldiers on my stage,
And I wonder if the others had seen the battle rage.
I think to them, it's history, just tombstones now exist.
And one last time I scan the fields and think what they have missed.

For Now

Beneath the limbs of history,
Protected year by year;
It sit's beneath the canopy
And fights to persevere.
A hundred years have passed it by
And time is it's reward,
For mossy limbs now match the walls
And silvered every board.
Some nights you smell the cook stove
And hear the voice of men,
Mingle with the children
As they all come home again.
On certain nights beneath the trees,
You might smell oil lamp
And swear someone is watching you
Out in the dew and damp.
There under limbs that know no time,
It's moss, a silvery crown,
Guard bravely o'er the metal roof
Until the house comes down.
And once again there is a loss,
For we have let it go
And in this hallowed spot in time
Some other thing will grow.
A parking lot, a new tract house,
A business, signs and posts
Will cover cracker history

And push out all the ghosts.
No more will whispers move by wind,
Nor moss be on display,
They've felled the trees, let houses rot
And ghosts have moved away.

Stuff

It has a "No Trespassing' sign
Nailed beside the door
And many who pass by see it,
But notice nothing more.

They know not of the heartache,
Of those that lived within,
The loneliness that fills the space
When death has claimed your kin.

When keeping pieces of your past
Has grown beyond control
And now the junk and trash has claimed
And taken o're the soul.

The house became part of despair
And crumbled with the load,
Filled with stuff and heartache,
Now piled by the road.

The woman now has passed her prime,
Was never someone's bride
And so she aged and kept her stuff
Close by her, right inside.

I do not know what fate awaits,
For time is not enough,
A lonely house is on the edge,
Her past, her life, and stuff.

Swamp Roach

Her hair fell like the mane
Of a wild mustang,
Tangled and burred
About her face and humped back.

Her eyes, green as the swamp pools
She splashed and danced in
And hooded by furry brows
that matched the grey of her head.

We called her Swamp Roach
Because we were children
and she was so different
And we were so young.

We called her Swamp Roach
And hid behind the cabbage palm,
To watch her cast spells
Over creatures we could not capture.

In the evenings while frogs croaked
And plunked from cypress logs,
We hid ourselves behind a tree
And watched her campfire grow dim in the night.

She appeared from the shadows of the hammock,
White dress dripping and clinging

To her humped back,
Strange words gurgling in her throat.
She pressed a picture against sagging breast.
There in the dying embers of a pine knot fire,
Amid bobcat and coon
She began her strange cotillion.

Holding to her picture,
She waltzed in her swamp ballroom,
Fire flies, her lanterns, sweeping tree limbs,
Webbed over by swamp spiders.

We called her Swamp Roach,
This old woman with scraggly hair and humped back,
Who danced with a picture
We never cared to see.

We called her Swamp Roach,
Because we were children,
And knew no better
And had no time to understand.

THE BROWARD COWARD

What makes a man turn into glue,
Not face the coming rendezvous,
Forget the training he has had,
Turn from cop, become a cad.
I've searched my mind, have not a clue.

Did legs begin to shake and fold,
He did not move, is what we're told.
He heard the shots that all rang out,
But he stood still, without a doubt,
A coward's stand down to behold.

While kids were dying in their rooms,
He stood outside among the booms,
He did not see the blood, the spatter,
Yet stood there frozen, did not matter
That school house was now a tomb.

Once the children, young and strong,
Were in the rooms where they belonged,
The cop retired on the spot,
Before the back up and the SWAT,
He retires, they do not,
There's something here that's very wrong.

Though doors were open, staircase towered,
He stood by, was not empowered,
A cop with pistol, just a con,
A casual cop, he looked upon
The scene that made him Broward's Coward.

Twas The Month Before Christmas

Twas the month before Christmas and all thru the house,
both they and the senate…quiet as a mouse.
They were adjourned without one little care
for all of them knew their check would be there.
The Congress were nestled, all snug in their beds,
while visions of staffers all danced in their heads.
Chuck readied himself with a little night cap
while Nancy was ready for a long winter's nap.
When out at the White House there arose such a clatter,
CNN and their ilk went to see what the matter.
Trump and Melania were there in a flash,
while CNN hoped they'd report on some trash.
The moon on the breast of the new fallen snow
made the cockroaches all stand out there below.
When what to my wondering eyes should appear,
but Franken and Conyers, both guzzling a beer.
There's an Uber driver so lively and quick,
I could see in the light, he had more than one chick.
More rapid than eagles, the dems quickly came.
Trump tweeted about them and called them by name.
Steny Hoyer, John Lewis, Debbie Wasserman Shultz,
Trump tweeted, "Now that's not all of the dolts."
Trump smiled as he thought of his beautiful wall
and them all behind it, once and for all.
But like surrounding a dung pile, the bugs and the flys

sent their stench wafting upwards, clouding the skies.
All the dem Congress was out in plain view,
Both of the Clinton's both Obama's there too.
I thought I was seeing a Saturday nite spoof.
Clinton was screaming, "I'll get you some proof."
Trump was shaking his head and 'bout to turn 'round
when Bernie and Rocket Man came with a bound.
He was dressed all in black from his head to his foot,
smelled like last year's fish dinner and covered in soot.
A bundle of rockets he had hung on his back,
he pulled launchers and matches from out of his sack.
Then Maxine's eyes twinkled and Schiff now so merry,
Barney Frank has come over with more than one fairy.
Pocahontas was given a present and bow,
wrapped neatly inside, John McCain, white as snow.
His eyes were a'blazin' and he gritted his teeth,
had a hundred, "VOTE NAY" glued to a wreath.
He had 'Prisoner of War' tattooed to his belly,
and he like the rest had brains made of jelly.
John Lewis was there, a fat, chubby ole elf,
and I laughed when I saw him in spite of myself.
He was blubbering some hate speech, no one knew what he said,
Trump just shook his head and went off to bed.
Trump spoke not a word, changed his mind, went to work,
tweeted something about there being more than one jerk.
He waved a good-by as McCain blew his nose
and marveled and watched as the bullshit just rose.
Trump went unto bed with his phone in his hand,
tweeted. "God Bless America" and "Save this great land."
But I saw him tweet out, before falling asleep,
Rocket Man is below, shaking hands with his sheep!

2017

The Phantom

The yanks called him the 'Devil Horse,'
That thundered through the night,
Black as coal from eyes to tail
With just a speck of white.

His eyes and nose were black as soot,
His hooves had not a crack,

His coat, his tack, his mane, his tail
Were dark as midnight black.
The wind would whip his battle flag
And blow his darkened mane,
His hooves would pound forgotten fields,
Though no one held the rein.
Tis strange at how he pranced and pawed
And screamed there in the night
And as he passed with shaking head
You'd hear the battle fight.
The smell of powder filled the air,
You'd hear the cannon's blast,
You'd hear the cries of fallen men
As bullets whistled past.
There under gray and smoke filled sky
He'd gallop or'e the ground,
I'm sure each time he thundered past
There were soldiers gathered 'round.
No rider ever held his reins,
No soldier sat upon,
As fast as he would gallop forth
The Devil Horse was gone.

The Spirits

Who can know a Southron's heart,
What makes it beat so fast,
While standing on the sacred ground
That honors Southron past.
Who can know the depths of pride,
To stand upon the ground
And wonder at the ghosts that watch,
The spirits gathered 'round.
The wind lay still as I stood there,
So few they'd been that come,
So few would stop to hear the guns,
The bugle, fife and drum.
I stood awhile, lost in my thoughts,
Rocked there to and fro,
Unaware that they were there…
The past of long ago.
I did not know they watched for me,
Were waiting till I came,
I did not see the line of gray
Next to the soldier's name.
I offered up a quick salute,
Left Southron flag in place
And did not notice breeze begin,
That blew around my face.
I turned but once and saw the flag,

Waving there that night,
Unaware of men in gray
That watched, just out of sight.
Soon I'll know the Southron wind
That touched my face and hair,
Were all the men that went before,
The ones I thought not there.
For though I came and stood alone
By monument and plaque,
The wind were whispers of the men
That all saluted back.

The Storm

Tomorrow night the wind will blow
And swirl 'round the edge,
And push against the worn boards,
That's holding to the ledge
Of being here, being gone,
A memory is all,
The rain will come, the wind will push,
Another home will fall.
Cypress planks will warp and pull,
While every rainy drip,
Will pull against the board and nail
Until it loses grip.
The metal roof will let in leaks
And slowly it will drown,
Another piece of all our past
Will lose and tumble down.

The Visitor

They board my doors to keep things out,
Perhaps to keep things in,
But still I see who passes by
Beneath my aged tin.
My days have all been long and hard,
Life never comes with ease,
So here I sit and watch the road
And peek beneath the trees.
One time an old man came and sat
Upon my old porch boards,
A life long lived sees many things
And has it's own rewards.
He bent and touched a brick or two,
Then piled them in a stack.
I didn't know until he spoke,
Then memories all rushed back.
I saw him as a little boy,
Years after I began,
Now here he sits upon my porch,
An old and aged man.
It was his great granddad that hewed
The mighty pine, so tall
And fashioned every piece of wood
That made up every wall.
He brushed his bibs and looked around,
His stacking was now through.

He sat awhile and swatted flies
Much like he used to do.
I don't watch time as others can,
Although I sometimes try,
He rubbed my boards with wrinkled hand
Till an hour passed him by.
Was then a youngster ambled in
And never looked around,
Not once looked up to see the man,
his eyes stayed on the ground.

Photo by Bob Shuker

He mumbled something, "Bout let's go,
the drive was much to far."
Said, "Momma's getting real mad
Out there in the car."
The old man winced as he stood up,
Held post so he could stand.

I saw the tear that trickled down,
Wiped by his wrinkled hand.
The grandson, not once tried to help,
Walked off like some young pup,
Stared at something in his hand
And never once looked up.
I slumber now to keep my strength,
It seems a heavy load,
But in the shade it's easier
To look back down the road.

The Kill Pen

I drop my head and snatch at weeds
And think of centuries gone,
before I ever knew this time,
was ever sat upon.
At night when winds begin to blow,
Skies free from light and bird,
I take a breath and lift my head
And listen to the herd
That race against the fiery wind,
That flames the drying grass;
I watch the young, I see the old
As they all gallop past.
Their nostrils flare to catch the wind,
I watch them rear and dance,
The colts and fillies frolic by,
The young ones paw and prance.
I watch them go to battle,
In breastplates etched in gold,
I see their frosty breath expel
There in the freezing cold.
They pull the carts full of your dead,
When pestilence abounds,
They've drown in mighty sailing ships,
In storms or run aground.
The herds have taken you out west,
Have helped all to explore,
Have cleared the mighty path for men

And carried them to war.
They've run your race and plowed your field,
Took bullets, arrows, lash,
Been wounded, broken, beaten down
With spurs and saber slashed.
We've raised your children patiently,
Allowed you freedom's ride
And partnered with the good and bad,
Allowed you by our side.
I nicker for the one I know,
Then drop my head to feed,
Not much is left amid the dust,
Just dirt, more dirt and weed.
I close my eyes and listen to
The sound of trucks arrive,
My pasture now is just a pen,
Some young, some just alive.
I slowly walk into the ring,
The bidding starts, then stops.
I'm startled at the echo there
As hammer quickly drops.
How fast the truck is ready, filled,
A stranger says, "Let's go,"
I look between the slats of death;
"Where is the one I know?"

A Woman's Thoughts in '64

There was a day we had both meat and grain,
And dances where we waltzed the night away,
But now there is no time to dance nor play.
I wonder if they'll ever be again.
It's been so long and memories will fade,
Like the trimmings of old, forgotten lace.
We live behind the shutters at our place.
We heard the troops were moving to invade
And women should be careful, not ignore
What old men from the guard had finally said,
"Get children in and lock the gate and door,
Hide all the horses that are finely bred,
Hide all your treasures underneath the floor.
There is no time to flee where others fled."

There is no time to flee where others fled,
We must move fast and hide with no delay,
For Sherman and his Bummers' on the way.
Where land was green, it now is running red.
I heard they hit Miss Hattie on a raid
And what they did was surely a disgrace.
They burned and looted with a lightening pace
And slashed her portraits with a soldier's blade,
Then dammed her and the South, oh how they swore,
You'd think in front of children they'd refrain,
But laughed and cussed the Southland even more.
They rifled all her shacks and burned the cane,

And said they'd burn the South from shore to shore.
When war is over, what will there remain?

When war is over, what will there remain,
Will we have milk enough to even pour?
I try to understand this yankee war.
I call my children and try to explain,
That soon we'll have no beans and hardly bread,
Nor wagons to take eggs to town to trade,
For soldiers hide in willowed glen and glade.
No one is safe as they have been before.
The Bible says that we live under grace,
Yet all the world is now in disarray;
Of human kindness there is not a trace,
This madness makes it hard for me to pray.
John Michael has become a stranger's face
And he and God both wear the coat of gray.

And he and God both wear the coat of gray.
I'm sure in heaven there is a brigade
Of angels praying for us, unafraid,
Thru morning, noon and night of every day.
At night when I am praying in my bed,
I think of those that have to soon been slain.
Tears well within my eyes from all the pain
Of thinking of our soldiers laying dead.
I wonder if somewhere, far out in space,
There is a special place without this gore,
Where people are not killing, all embrace
And watch together as the white doves soar.
Somewhere there will be vultures to give chase,
The lamb somewhere will hear the lion roar.

I play no cards, but know God holds the ace
And only he can lead us all ahead,

I know where he is leading, where he's led,
That life is more than just an earthly race.
I know in heaven sins have all been paid
And yankees then will know the South's disdain,
For rivers will run free without blockade
And food enough for bellies to contain.
But I am hungry and must find some shade,
There was a day we had both meat and grain.

Beer Cans and Dead Dogs

Fall must be closing in for I can see
The rooting of the grass along the road,
Bucks have scraped their velvet on a tree
While hunters leave the woods like a commode.

Yes, hunters have come back in heavy force,
They hide in trees and blend in with the logs.
It's the time of year when wives think of divorce
And I grow tired of beer cans and dead dogs.

Every hundred feet there is a place
Where six packs are dispensed along the side,
The roads out here are really a disgrace,
While on the wind, McDonald wrappers glide.

Their dogs don't know to look before they leap,
They cross the road where deer have gone before.
I guess the price of dogs is very cheap
And where they get them, there is always more.

The hunters can't be bothered to live here,
It's miles from work and way out, much to far,
Not near enough to buy their shells and beer
And to far to tell their tales in a bar.

They pay no heed to posted signs we buy,
Domestic pigs become their wild hogs.
When leaves start turning in the autumn sky,
It's the season of the beer cans and dead dogs.

Wild Moors and Willowed Glen

He sang her ballads of the night,
Of hedgerows made of stone that he had made
And castles that would dizzy in their height,
He sang of far off lands and each crusade.

His voice would rise and fall with every note
That his fingers fretted on the mandolin,
She'd see his monsters floating in the moat
And blush when he would sing to her of sin.

He sang her ballads of the night,
When candles lent their shadows to the wall.
He sang of kisses so polite
That the mandolin could not be heard at all.

He'd sing of bogs and wispy, willowed glen,
Of knights in polished amour, debonair,
But the fingers that played the mandolin
Never once touched the maiden, young and fair.

He sang her a hundred months of songs,
And through the years their hair both turned to gray.
He never kissed the maiden though he longs
For the beauty of his life that passed away.

Now through the wild moor the wind has blown,
He sings to keep her memory in his sight.
He touches her sweet name upon the stone
And plays her favorite ballads in the night.

Strangers have been heard to hear her sigh,
On stormy nights you hear his mandolin,
In a misty haze of years long since gone by,
You remember wild moors and willowed glen.

The Unexpected Guest

The weeds have claimed allotted plot
And time has hastened in it's rot,
Metal now is bent and broke,
Home to spiders, not to folk.
Now sadness has consumed this spot.

I look and touch the silvered board,
It's windows, roof in one accord,
The porch is sagging just a bit,
A few floor boards are weak and split,
But fighting on is its reward.

Reflections of the years gone past,
Its memories, so long and vast
Hold sadness with the strength of Rome,
No ancient columns, just a home
That now is crumbling fast.

I strain to hear the whispers there,
To write something that I could share.
Perhaps they have no words to say
In this home so old and gray,
It seems as if no ones aware.

The breeze picks up and cools the shade
While summer's heat begins to fade.

I find myself alone despite
Birds flitting in the shafts of light,
I think perhaps I've over stayed.

The spirits have refused request,
It does no good to stay, protest.
The secrets will remain within,
Covered by the rusty tin,
Not wanting unexpected guest.

Photo by Andrea Sadock

The Voice and Time of Nature

What men decide they do not want,
Nature claims it back,
Weeds and ivy take it or'e
And crawls in every crack.

The clearing now becomes a glade
To spiders, coons and snakes
And when a family walks away
Nature steals and takes.
The whitewash of the old front porch
Is home to squirrel and owl
And there amid the glade and glen
The bobcat, panther prowl.
The silence of the palms and ferns
Swish there in gentle breeze
And slowly now old house gives way
And dies there 'neath the trees.
There are no shouts from playing kids
And not a dog to bark,
Though shadows dance and claim their space
When daylight turns to dark.
The winds of hurricanes and time
Together meets, prepares,
What man decides he does not want
Nature calls it theirs.

On A Rainy Day

Was on a dark and dreary morn, in woodland very dense,
Full of trees that drizzled down with rain upon the tents.
A respite from the battlefield, before the next campaign,
Their fires flickered, gave no warmth and wavered in the rain.
A dank and marshy, muddy swamp would have to be crossed o'er,
To meet up with the regiment that crossed it days before.
Cedar Creek lay to the north, a bridge at Fishers Hill,
Was on the minds of all the men that stomped against the chill
And lit a smoke from dampened match and knew what lay ahead,
Their calloused hands yearned to hold a loved one there instead,
Of straining mules thru mud and mire while stomachs tie in knots,
From hunger that would never cease and ducking deadly shots.
A letter home was quickly wrote, of death, of love, of pain,
Then marching on, they disappeared in drizzly morning rain.

I watched them cross the foggy swamp, ghost soldiers on my mind,
I knelt and picked up smoldering stick from fire left behind.
Go forth, go forth, my southron men. I pray you all survive,
For death is but a resting place, your spirit is alive.
I smell your smoke left in the air, there's no way to explain;
When sun is bright and air is warm, I feel the driving rain.
Your flag flies in my heart and soul, your face I'll always see.
You watch for me, for I am there, the smoke beneath the tree.

When The Welcome Sign Is Not Out

I can almost see the spirits,
Thru wavy glass of time,
I push against the cobwebs
That spiders used to climb.
The trees have fallen quiet,
Their leaves are still, except
The scurry of a lizard
As I started up the step.
The gray of all the old plank walls
Were rough all 'way across
And in the shadows of the porch
Blended with the moss.
An old chair sat there on the floor,
Covered o're in dust,
A door knob that locked years ago,
Eaten 'way by rust.
Yet still it held and kept me out...
Or locked the spirits in,
The windows all were painted shut,
The curtains, old and thin.
I pressed against the wavy glass
And closed my eyes to squint,
But all I left behind me there
Was nose and fingerprint.
I thought I heard a muffled noise,
The faint sound of a scratch,
I tried the doorknob one more time

And heard the click of latch.
I knew right then, as sure as not,
I wasn't wanted here,
This old home place was still a home
And spirits made that clear.
I slowly walked back to the fence,
For hour was getting late,
I stood and studied silver boards,
Then slowly closed the gate.
I thought the fence had kept cows out,
But that and the old key,
Were meant to keep the stranger out
And meant for even me.
My mind took notes as I stood there,
The boards, the rusty tin;
I realized the fence, the lock
Kept all the spirits in.
I smiled and thought I understood,
This home place had its day
And who wants strangers walking in..
I'd want it the same way.
Was then I heard the old door creak,
I turned around to see,
A child, a woman at the door
Looking back at me.
I walked back to the shaded porch,
She motioned me, come in,
Her clothes threadbare and tattered some
They both were whisper thin.
She brushed the dust from off the chair
And tried to hide her frown,
The child held tightly to her dress,
She asked me to sit down.
It was a moment 'for she spoke,

Her voice was soft and low,
She pulled her child close to her
And spoke of long ago.
"He said that he was coming back,
That I should never leave,
Now it's been years since he has left
And everyday I grieve.
My shelves have emptied long ago.
You must think I so rude,
But look around, we've nothing left,
No water, clothes, no food..
You see it was a few years back,
When others just like you
Came and pushed the old door in,
Took all when they were thru.
They rifled thru my dresser there,
Broke canning jars and glass,
When they left, what was left
Was nothing more than trash.
We locked the door and locked the gate
And never had a doubt
That he would come and rescue us,
We never once went out."
I reached out then to touch her hand,
Both bowed their head and knelt
And as my hand touched only air,
And mist was all I felt.
I shuddered at what I had seen
And what my ears had heard.
I sat a moment to recall
The softness of her word.
I knew she would be waiting still,
I never had a doubt,
I locked the door before I left

To keep the strangers out.
I turned just once and locked the gate,
I left her to be free,
I knew the fence and knew the lock
Was meant for even me.

Unspoken Words

When did he ever say he loved me too?
Was it before my memory grew dim?
He knows the one I love and it's not him.
I saved the folded flag that covered you.
He saw me once beside your flowered grave
And never knelt to wipe away a tear.
I tried to love again, but now I fear,
The memories of you are all I save.
He does not know the nights you come to me
And slip beside me while I am asleep.
He thinks he owns me and I am not free,
He thinks that I am his to hoard and keep.
Oh how I begged to go with you, to flee
this place of sadness where he hears me weep.

This place of sadness where he hears me weep,
A realm that I have built for me alone,
Where mountains have already grown too steep
And softness in a heart has turned to stone.
I've heard men say that war is just a game,
That governments all play from time to time,
But now I'm left with mountains I can't climb
And love is not a thing that I can claim.
I see the stars that glitter in the sky
And wonder if there ever is a link.
Between the words hello and then goodbye.
All night I wait for you and then I think

Of ways to cross and ways that I might try.
I wait for courage...then I mix a drink.

I wait for courage, then I mix a drink
To ponder in my head what must be done.
I look for staying reasons, but there's none
And shiver as I waver at the brink.
He's sleeping now, I hear him softly snore,
He can not own what never could be his
And can not understand just what this is,
This pain that leads me down death's corridor.
Perhaps I'll leave a note to tell him how
I'm leaving and that I could never stay,
Though he loved me all his heart would allow,
The emptiness was leading to decay.
Plans are made, I'm feeling better now,
All must be carried out with no delay.

All must be carried out with no delay,
Before the bourbon shows what I have planned.
I'll leave him dignity, my wedding band
And tell him he's no longer in my way.
The stone that covers you is very cold
And flowers have been scattered by the wind,
My fingers then were bleeding, knuckles skinned.
I look for you to kiss and finally hold.
Your flag! It lays forgotten on my bed,
I'll need it for this final rendezvous.
The bourbon is now throbbing in my head,
My plan must not be stopped, be carried through.
What was it that my husband once had said?
"When did he ever say he loved me too?"

When Once There Was A Lane

I sit to near the road today,
It wasn't always so,
My trees once shaded old dirt lane
That led here long ago.
My timbers once were straight and long,
My porch was welcome shade
And I could see right through the trees,
Those coming up the grade.
Back then the wagons hauled the load
And mules were bred tough,
When master sat here with his pipe
And mistress with her snuff.
But those were days of bygone years,
Of long johns and night gown.
I watched the children grow and leave
And move on into town.
Years ago the smokehouse burned,
Demise is now complete
And soon my rooms just heard the sound
Of old and shuffling feet.
My chimneys claimed by birds and bats,
My walls are growing mold.
My boards dry out and pull at nails,
My rooms have grown cold.
But under boards that hold my porch
And in between the cracks,
There's marbles of another time,

A horseshoe and some jacks.
Just little things that only I
Know of and now hold dear,
When paint was fresh and timbers straight,
When people once lived here.
My lane is gone and asphalt now
Leads past horizon, sky,
There are no mules, no creaking loads
That slowly pass on by.
I hold together best I can
In cold and when it's warm
And brace myself against the years
That bring on gale and storm.
The years have grown quiet now
And though I still remain.
I curse the asphalt right out front
And wish for shaded lane.

Photo by Linda Sanders

Who Is To Know?

She sat alone out on the porch
With hen there in her lap
While both hands held the bony bird
So neither wing could flap.
She watched the far horizon,
Saw dust clouds in the air
And touched the old hen tightly
As she rocked there in her chair.
The men had long since marched to war
And now she was alone.
The wild hogs had ate the greens
That grew next to her home.
The corn had tasseled long ago,
Yet ears of corn were rare,
Flour, salt had long since gone
And left her cupboards bare.
The old home once had seen the growth
Of boys to fine, young men,
Now all there was to fill this space
Was her and bony hen.
She watched the path that they had gone,
Now tracks of panther, coon
And nightly prayed for all her boys
To be returning soon.
The floorboards creaked each time she rocked
And soon her rocking slowed,
She cupped one hand around an eye
to see far down the road.

The chicken struggled to get down,
But soon gave up the fight,
The woman just stared down the road
And held the chicken tight.
She sat alone out on the porch
With hen there in her lap
And softly rubbed the old hen's neck
Before she made it snap.
They found her there a month ago,
Her sons still off to war
And there she sat in rocking chair
With feathers on the floor.
They say hers sons have come and left,
The living was too hard
And some have sworn on many days
There's chickens in the yard.
They say a woman once walked in,
Scared womenfolk and men,
She walked across the parlor floor
And held a bony hen.
Through the years a few have come,
But none has ever stayed,
They hear a rocker on the porch
As daylight starts to fade.
Now who's to know what is the truth,
It's many years since then,
Yet even now upon the porch
Are feathers of a hen.

Suffer the Little Children

A child is left at home alone
With monsters hiding under chairs,
With TV on and telephone,
With no one there to hear his prayers,
He hides himself against the wall.
This little child, so young, so small,
Cries silently with unleashed tears,
Sees demon eyes and devil sneers
All hiding in his darkened space.
He prays his momma soon appears,
But who shall kiss this little face?

A child conceived in mother's youth,
She's told it's not a child yet.
The movement in her knows the truth,
We teach no sin, have no regret.
The baby burns and fingers grasp,
The mother never hears the gasp.
Another baby never born
Is heaped upon the burned, the torn
And still we teach it's no disgrace.
We want the rose without the thorn,
But who shall kiss this baby's face?

A child is slapped when milk is spilled,
"Dumb, stupid," are the words he knows.

A loving spirit has been stilled
With broken bones as child grows.
As thoughtless words tear down, degrades,
A child lives here with pulled down shades.
The little child, now black and blue
Has lived through one more rendezvous.
A child has grown with no embrace,
His innocence stares back at you.
But who shall kiss this child's face?

The Ash Heap of History

Some call it the ash heap of history,
I call it heartbreakingly sad,
I think under all of those ashes
Are houses I wish that I had.
There under the smoldering embers
Are timbers all hewn by hand,
Fingers of fire lapped at the walls
Till it crumbled, unable to stand.
It pops and it crackles at midnight,
Fire knows not a width or a length,
Hart pine, seasoned by centuries
Sizzles and gives up it's strength.
Beneath the ashes of history,
I hear the long ago sigh,
When homes of the crackers and planters,
lifted high into fiery sky.
Who now walks where scorched house was standing?
There's no sign of the home or it's folk,
Yet some still feel a sad quiver
And some smell that long ago smoke.

When The Last One Has Left

I stepped unto the old porch floor,
Each step was careful choice,
I let my eyes adjust a bit
And listened for a voice.
The termite dust was everywhere,
They'd eaten most the door,
The chimney was half crumbled 'way
In piles upon the floor.
But yet the beauty of this place
Had called me further in,
I stepped across a line of ants
And over twisted tin.
I bent and picked an old brick up,
Ran fingers o're its sides
And wondered at who last lived here
And who it was decides
That locking doors won't hold much in
And now it's all okay
To walk across the old plank floors
And sadly move away.
I thought about the children here
And prayed in their behalf
And strain to hear from long ago
A child's happy laugh.
An emptiness from years gone by
Has filled my heart and mind
And fills my soul with sadness

that it was left behind.
The trees have crept almost inside,
Their branches rub and chafe,
Protected by their limbs of time
They keep the old home safe.
The metal roof is sagging some,
Foundation still in place,
And as I stare at what once was,
It's hard to leave this place.
The solace of a hundred years
Has beckoned me to stay
And burn a memory in my mind
Of beauty in decay.
What year was it the last man left?
Did he look around before,
He touched the doorknob of his life
And walked on out the door.

Angry? Not Hardly

Angry isn't quite the word
I'd use on me today,
This country has now lost it's mind
And stands in disarray.
Now what the hell, we don't want cops,
And do away with I.C.E?
Do all the stupid people now
Believe we all are nice?
Why let the beggars all come in,
Give them a helping hand,
After all, they just want work
And have no more demands.
Let China screw us all they want,
Let muslim's make the law,
And golly, let us all stand back
And worship them in awe.
Let's get the baby factories,
Birth centers in each zone,
Their birthing all our citizens,
While we kill all our own.
Who needs a gun now-a-days,
We must all learn retreat
And look the other way I guess
When blood pools in the street.
MS 13 is all our friends,
Pelosi says they're good,
And now-a-days we must stand by

And love those in the hood.
"Pay up white man, it's all your fault,"
White privilege, they say.
How in the world would they all live
If we all went away?
No.... angry isn't quite the word
Closer...slobbering mad
I watch the country's down hill slide
And remember what we had.

One Potato, Two Potato

At recess, he was bullied from the swing,
Pointed at and laughed at by the girls;
He told the teacher only that one time.
While she was grading papers in the shade
She never looked while he was pushed away
And never hugged him when she had the time.
The glasses, thick as bottles on his face,
Often slipped down on his freckled nose
And never helped him as he fought to read.
The C's and D's, they often looked alike
And 6s and 9s were often upside down,
By eight the struggle stopped, he did not read.
His science books had pictures he could see,
One celled creatures floating in the swamp
And from this murky place all life began,
From fish to bird, then monkey, then a man.
He thought how far he's come from that one bang,
From nothing, then the universe began.
The frog lay slit and pegged upon the board,
His innards neatly marked and pinned in place,
He's done his best and passed this only once.
He learned of war from history picture books
And studied broken bodies on the shore.
He asked his father questions only once.
In health class he was taught you could decide,
To love a woman or to love a man,
That only you knew when the time was right.

They took the boys aside and taught them how
To use all of the gadgets for safe sex,
That it was up to them to get it right.
He yearned to touch a lock of golden hair
And wondered if a kiss had any taste,
He asked her once, but then she changed her mind.
He knew a baby never would be born
Even if he did not get it right.
 A fetus had no life or human mind.
He sits there on a swing from long ago
And watches buses pull into the school,
His face is rigid as kids play and run.
The glasses have grown foggy on his face,
The cross-hairs have been leveled more than once,
He fires and watches all the children run.

Written after a school shooting in the 80's. Trying to figure out what could make a child into a killer.

Two Ladies

They sit upon their shaded porch,
A respite from the day,

Living history under eaves,
There sitting on display.

They looked out on the fields and trees,
The land that held their soul,
Two ladies resting from their work,
The young of long ago.
Their apron stained with this and that,
Their gray heads both held high,
Memories of a hundred years
Relived there in their eyes.
The wrinkled hands that held the plow
In furrows long and straight,
Are hands that cooled a fevered brow
And filled a supper plate.
The lines of life are etched on them,
Their lives about complete,
Two ladies rest there in the shade,
A respite from the heat.
Their cradles rocked so long ago,
To tunes we'll never know,
Two ladies rest upon the porch,
The young of long ago.

Gone Is Forever

The planks have seen the many years
Of cypress on its wall
And heard the laughter, seen the tears
Of those that walked its hall.
The trees have tried to keep it safe,
As though they were afraid,
Their spreading limbs assured the home
A place there in the shade.
They watched the children in the yard,
The mule behind the plow
But now waits for the buzz of saw,
For no house stands there now.
Though while it stood and fought the fight,
Seems no one had a plan,
It fought for life behind the trees,
Against the time of man.
The mighty winds of hurricanes
Pushed against its sides,
Yet battered through the years it stood;
Until someone decides
That this old home has no more right
To stand and must be gone,
Dismembered, torn and finally burned,
While ghosts of old looked on.
Still now I hear the families past,
The mules snort and bray
And sadly see them one by one,

Till all have moved away.
In years to come how will one know
Of former pioneer
And who will grieve what we have lost,
When beauty once stood here?

Cathy asked that I write about an old home that no longer stands. This is a tribute to that old place.

Photy by Cathy Cooper Sharp

A Hundred Years Of Footsteps

A hundred years of footsteps
Have walked upon the floor,
Opened windows for a breeze
And stood there in the door.
They rested there upon the porch
And watched the daylight fade
And in the heat of summer sun,
Would rest there in it's shade.
Now the floors begin to sag,
In places rotted through,
Yet still it stands fighting on
For one last rendezvous.
The dust blows in from off the road,
Through casements with no glass,
Yet still the house holds to the land
And fights the years that pass.
Damp and dew have left their mark,
Where bugs and spiders crawl,
Mold has claimed the ceiling
And is growing down the wall.
The boards have pulled the nails loose
And coons have made their way
Into the dark recesses
Of this old home in decay.
Though dead leaves cover rusted roof,
Though walls be warped and cracked,
It stands through storms and driving rain

And challenged all attacks.
But years have stolen strength and grit
And time is not it's friend,
While it fights bravely to hold on,
Time waits for it to end.
I stroke the old, porch floor boards,
As if my touch will soothe,
Where a hundred years of footsteps
Have worn the old boards smooth.
The ferns will creep unto the porch
And trees may one day fall
And nature will claim back her space,
With no house here at all.

Home

Saying Good-bye To A Friend

How could I know that soon I would not need
a reason to be buying oats and hay;
that morning and the nightly feeding time
would be stopped in less than just a week away.
How could I know that soon your head would lay
out in the dirt; I held you on my knees
and whispered to you of a resting place
as I said good by beneath the winter trees.
I talked of times when we were both so young
and knew all of the trails, both far and near;
I knew this day would come yet did not know
what I would feel when it was finally here.
I pray you knew no thunder when it came,
that eyes were closed and that you did not see;
for your labored breath to cover rifle shot,
for he was also shooting part of me.
Old Joe, I sit and hold part of your tail,
that I cut when we were talking in the shade;
I hope the trail you're on is evergreen,
as you walk into the willowed glen and glade.
Stop beside the creek bank where we rode,
like we've done in all the years before,
and wait for me my friend, in shady lane
and together we will ride to heaven's shore.

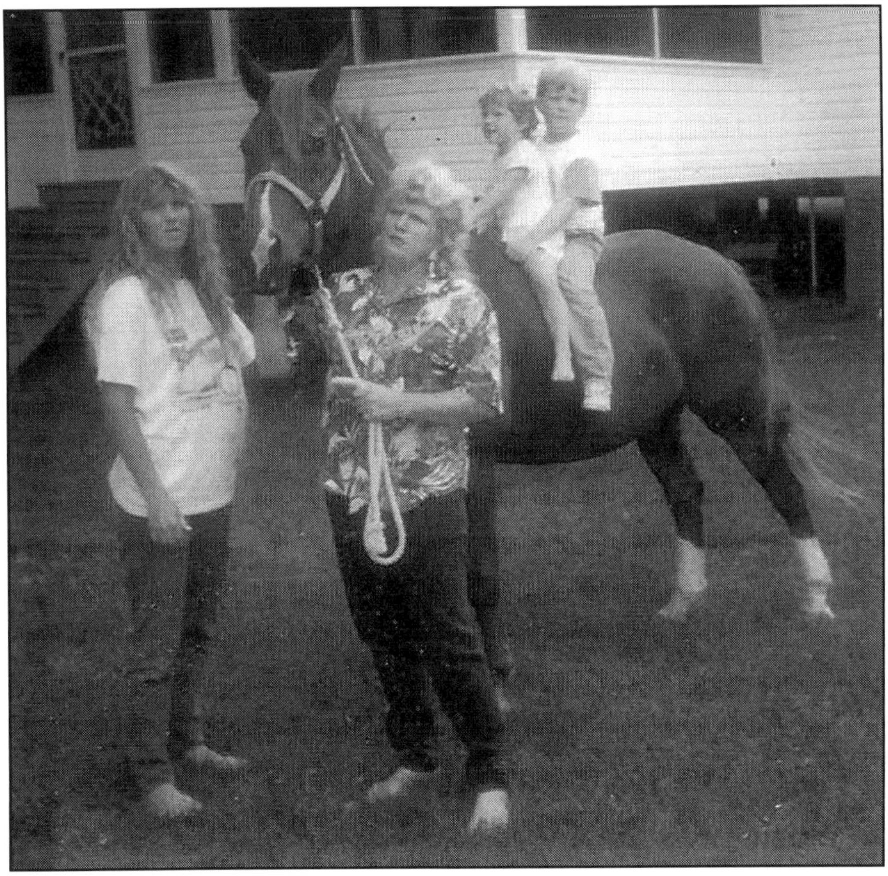

Brightly Boxed and Bowed

The Christmas cards began to arrive today,
I taped them all along the dining hall.
The tree is up, the house in disarray,
With boxes to be wrapped, both large and small.

"To my Daughter." was the card you had sent.
I smiled at all the frilly words it said.
I straightened out a corner that was bent
and touched the Christ child there upon his bed.

You fussed about the gifts you gave each year
And say, "They have to be exactly right."
The car was loaded and you got them here
All brightly wrapped and bowed by Christmas night.

I mix a little coke, a little rum
And listen to the grandkids by the tree.
I watch the door and know that you won't come
And wonder if tonight you're missing me.

There's one gift left, a tiny, tattered bow,
When it's opened Christmas will be done.
The name tags blurred with ink from years ago,
Within, a card from nineteen ninety-one.

"To my Daughter," was the card you sent.
I smiled at all the frilly words it said.
The box by now was crumpled, corner bent,
The Christmas wrapping taped where it was shred.

You're now with angels that were there that night,
Though ashes have been spread upon the sea.
I watch the stars that give the heaven light
And hold the Christmas card you sent to me.

1996

The Man In My Life

He does not know my soldiers have his face,
he thinks I am a dreamer.
Perhaps, but the image is always his.
The tattered, gray coat is upon his back
And the boots that march the weary path of war
Are his, not a stranger I could never know.
The trembling hand that holds the sword,
The spurs that urge his horse forward,
The blood that spills upon the ground
Are all his.

He does not know the moments I stop
To remember the smell of him,
To call back a moment of passion.

He calls me a castle builder,
A vacationer in a land of romance and legend.
But he is my slayer of dragons
And while my crusader sleeps
I watch the slow rise and fall of his chest.
There in virtue in veined hands
That even in sleep reach out for mine.
I press his hand to my cheek
And hold this moment
For a time he is not here.

I wonder which night did we sleep,
What night did we go to bed so young
And wake so old.

But he need not worry
For my soldiers are young.
My commanders are dashing
And ride white stallions
Into the thick smoke of the fray.
It is his steely eyes that study battle maps
And writes home of maneuvers.
It is always him that sneaks into my writing,
Into my daydreams, into my reading.

At least I think it's him.

Two Sisters

My sister talked of moving home, so we were on the hunt,
Looking for a place to buy with oaks just right out front.
We were lost, but looking for a certain house she found,
While she was reading dusty signs, I was looking 'round.
"Did you see that?" I heard her say, as husband drove on by,
"Back her up and let me out," came my quick reply.
We stood a moment at the road, the tangled weeds had grown.
I went forth while she stayed back and left me there alone.
For sisters have a special way, of reading thoughts unsaid
And she knew well why I was there and thoughts now in my head.
I stepped thru ferns and broken boards that lay upon the ground.
The moment that I took a breath, the spirits gathered 'round.
They circled me and pulled me near, I felt their hand on mine.
I took a breath and looked ahead and stepped back into time.
The weathered boards, now warped with age, it's all a sad lament,
From old bedsteads to rotten stairs, to metal, twisted, bent,
All reappeared as though I was, the first and not the last
Of visitors that entered in, a stranger from the past.
Two ladies with their bonnets tight, covered face and hair,
Took my hand and slowly led me up the wooden stair.
The rooms were clean and tidy, just four rooms very small,
A wash basin, a bureau and a bed against the wall.
The bed was just a set of springs with mattress and no frame
And thru the bedroom window, sweet smell of jasmine came.

The parlor held the pictures of both women and their men.
Stern and steady was the look they captured way back then.
The fireplace had long been cold, with wood stacked by it's side
Chairs were placed around the hearth for warmth it could provide.

Trenton

Open windows let in breeze, while jasmine filled the air,
It slipped about the picture frames, it wafted or'e the chair.
We stood there at the window, in the shade of towering oak.
I strained to hear their every word they both so softly spoke.
They led me back unto the porch, to stairs I stand upon,
The smell of jasmine swirled 'round, then both of them were gone.
The walls again are falling down, it's sad to see decay,
I stay a moment longer and smell jasmine far away.
That too, so quickly disappeared, a call came from my spouse
I turned to leave and look again, to find my sister's house.
We finally found the right road sign, less than a mile away,
I got to tour an old homestead and she bought one today.
My heart so often breaks at sights, forgotten homes alone,
But sadness turned to joy today, my sister's moving home.
That night while laying in my bed, I thought, now life is fair,
My sister's coming home again and there's jasmine in the air.

Thoughts on turning 70

You know what really makes me mad?
When grandkids think you're old,
When really your not good for much,
Except for growin' mold.
To them you never rode a horse,
That did much more than walk
And often you begin to think
You can't chew gum and talk.
They weren't around to see you ride
Or take a daring chance,
And never think you had a horse
That reared or even danced.
But mostly it's the apathy,
Much more than I deserve,
I now am older, walking slow
And lost some of my nerve.
But now it's time, perhaps to give
My grandkids one last clue;
There was a day I did it all
When I was young like you.
I rode the ones that bucked and reared,
Rode straight and some that spinned,
I rode without a saddle then
And often raced the wind.
I felt the mane blow in my face,
The bit against the teeth,
I felt the power, held in check,

The horse just underneath.
I saw the ground go whizzing by,
I'd slacken hold on rein,
I'd cluck and slap him on the neck,
Put face into his mane.

But being fair, time comes to steal
And one night makes a trade,
And gives you age and snowy hair
And tries then to persuade
That growing old is not so bad,
It's slow to start, begin,
Your rides are short, your knees now ache
And old age creeps on in.
And soon the day has finally come,
It's awful, sad and cold,
When grandkids think you can't do much
For you have grown old.

I hope there will be one last ride,
While I am still around;
I'll loose the reins, give him his head
And gallop o'er the ground.
And one day if my name comes up,
They'll tell them all with pride,
The memories we shared that day,
On Mamaw's favorite ride.

The Spider Path

He shushed his sister into silence.
Her scrunched up face made no noise,
But it drove him crazy.
He led the way with a stick,
"My spider stick,"
Yet before the walk was through
It would swipe trees, become a saber,
Point out deer tracks,
Aim menacingly at his sister
And knock down a dozen spider webs.

We would sit on tree logs.
He would talk of wolves,
Of going to Alaska.
Though his eyes have only seen eight years
And mine forty more,
I see his wolves and his dreams.
I tuck this moment away
For I know he is leaving me,
Getting to old for hugs and things.

We three walk the lane to the old house.
They scurry under wire fences
While I fit between rusty barbs.
We have been there once a month
For five years, but young eyes
See new things in old objects.

Once again she is shushed into silence
For perhaps a ghost can be conjured up,
But only if there is quiet,
And only if he is the leader.

They climb warped boards of the cattle pen.
He points to the clearing where deer graze,
She pulls at a nail that has caught her.
We have talked, he and I
And I realize my granddaughter
Has taken the walk, but not the time.
I hold her hand and allow her to chatter
About childish things,
For she is only five,
Much to young to knock down spider webs.

Childhood to Manhood

He lay there silent, not yet stiff
And I stopped dead, afraid as if
My faltering steps would leave a track,
While cries were raised to bring him back.
But there he lay, his eyes alert,
His body quiet, well past hurt
And as I knelt in disbelief,
I touched his face and felt the grief
Of child's pain at such a loss,
For I was grown, yet stepped across,
The chasm that was in between
And once again I was the teen
That knelt beside a dying friend,
A child that could not comprehend.
But soon a grandson, home from school
Would learn of life, unjust and cruel
And I would have to do my part
In breaking faith and breaking heart.
I prayed for words to not destroy
 the memories of a little boy.
I slowly rose to dig the hole
With shaking hand and forced control.
I pushed aside my childish ache,
For soon my grandson's heart would break.
There is no comfort, yet somehow,
My life has come full circle now.
I know he'll stand in disbelief

And wipe the tears of childhood grief.
In years to come he'll know dismay,
He'll search his soul for things to say,
When his young child will say goodbye,
To beloved dog about to die.
No words of comfort can prepare,
We've given hearts for dogs to tear.

The Final Trail

The sun is high and heat drifts 'cross the grass, shimmers into hazy lines of warmth; you spend most days around the stable door, begging for the tidbits from the barn. You and I have seen the seasons pass and rode the trails of youth that we both loved; I've raised my kids and theirs, but so have you and now the gray has silvered both our hair. The saddle squeaks in places not before, reins and bridles long have been replaced; your darkened eyes have seen the start of blue for cataracts are stealing both our sights. The smell of hay and leather fill the barn. I feel your nose so gentle on my cheek. Thirty some odd summers come and gone, and you and I both feel the same ole creak. The vet sees you and doctors call me in, with you it's knees and kidneys, me, the heart, the outsides good but insides have grown old and I know this living world is not our home. So Joe, let's take another ride again. We'll feel the wind blow through your mane and mine. We'll leave them hoof prints on the sandy road to let them know that you and I are gone.

Cleaning Day At The Barn

I flicked the lights on in the barn
A day or two ago,
There were saddles stacked on boxes
And junk from head to toe.
My bridles lay there on a chair,
Reins tangled in a knot,
Jumbled in a messy mass
Of things that I'd forgot.
My husband helped me pull stuff out,
A daughter's couch and chair,
The things I stored for all my kids
Left no space anywhere.
I checked for spiders, carefully,
Made sure that all had died,
Then took the boxes from the barn
And stacked them all outside.
I soaped up all my saddles,
Untangled bridle reins,
Separated brush and comb,
Windexed the window panes.
I swept the floor and pushed the dust
Into a growing pile,
Then marveled at the space I found,
I had a center aisle.
I leaned against an empty wall,
Propped feet up on the hay
And noticed all the junk I moved

Was just ten feet away.
I opened boxes, taking time
To remember what was there,
It took more time than I had thought
So retrieved the creaky chair.
Shirts my grandson had once worn
When he was one or two,
A lock of daughter's golden hair,
A tiny, toddler shoe.
Nothing here I could throw out
So I stacked the stuff between
Saddles, bridles, a chair or two,
But at least the floor was clean.

A Gleaning of Memories

It was his 50th reunion
And the wrinkles of old age
Fell away like frosted leaves
In a January wind.
He talked less of operations
And more of high school ball,
Less of sick friends
And more of memories.

Hands that opened lockers
Those long fifty ago years
Now gently touched street signs
That brought remembrances
Into stories of sodas and first kisses.
Together we walked the avenues of his youth
And I saw a vision of the young boy
That is my father.

He stood before a porched house,
The home of his grandfather,
A man I barely remembered
And greatly feared.
He spoke of his mother, of Parkinson's Disease,
Of stickball in the street.
I listened to him on stairs
I learned to climb 48 years before.

But it was a potato peeler
That allowed eyes to be rubbed.
He talked again of his mother,
The school cafeteria where she worked,
Where we now stood.
I saw the tears of a young boy,
Reliving the ghosts of a long ago childhood.

He is my father,
This man who holds phantoms inside
And does not speak often.
But today spirits touched and we were together,
Gathering memories for the time
He will again talk of operations.

Unsaid Words To A Dead Mother

In the light of shadowed morning
I knew darkness so thick and black,
So heavy upon my heart,
It fought against separating
As I passed through.
There amid lambs and cherubs
It gleamed from the other side of my darkness,
White, small and innocent,
One rose upon the cover.
The preacher said his words,
Words I did not hear
Nor yet can recall.
I lingered there
With my hand upon the casket,
Sons are not meant to die so young.
I felt your arm around me,
Though I didn't tell you,
Your strength helped
As I walked thru the darkness
That speaks of death.
But now you also have gone,
Slipped away without warning,
Not telling me your good night kiss
Would be the last.
Where do I go now?
For the tides of the St. John
Have taken you to unknown places,

Scattering your ashes among fish and sea bird,
Sending memories in a million directions.
You did not know your son
Would follow so soon in death,
That I would need your strength,
For sons are not meant to die so young.
Perhaps it's better you did not see
His hands shake, his body tremble.
For who can understand death
Except those who are dying?
When the moon pulls
At the tides of the St. John,
Who will know you are there?
Your son and mine received a stone,
But you chose the watery grave,
Leaving no place to grieve.
Yet perhaps the fish and seabird know
And will tell their young
This is a hallowed place,
that a mother sleeps beneath
And her child weeps on the bank.

Dolls

Her eyes have seen the years go by,
In her corner by the door,
her arms hang lifeless by her side,
In her clothes from years before.

A lifeless thing out on display,
The eyes that only stare,
Yet rosy cheeks still sneak a peek,
Next to her matted hair.
I think of all the little girls,
The tom-boy and the lass,
Who might have held or picked her up,
In moments of the past.
Now here she sits thru days, thru years,
And guards the old wood door,
Thru ghostly visits, stormy nights
In clothes from long before.

We all know this doll has a name,
Yet no one holds her tight,
Her skin is cracked, her eyes glow red,
Her hair as black as night.
While her eyes blink and though she talks,
Her dress is ashen gray
And all the kids that come around
Will run the other way.
So mostly she sits in the dark,
Above the closet floor
And waits to let her red eyes blink
Behind the closet door.

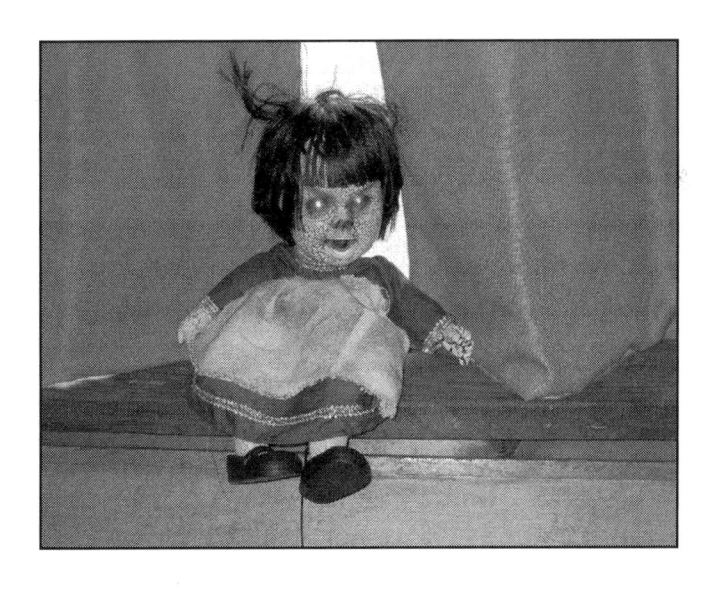

And now this doll forever swings
On ropes she can not climb,
She blankly stares at all who pass,
A prisoner in her time.
She looks as though she just escaped
The darkness of a tomb

And though she swings, she beckons all
To join her in the gloom.

"Come near, my friend and join me,
There's others I can bring,"
And thru the years she asks them all
To join her on the swing.

Now this doll knows all their tales,
Her name, Lucinda Lee,
I smile at her and dust her off,
For she belongs to me.

Lucinda says they often talk,
But secrets she will keep,
She whispers to me, "Dolls come forth,"
When we are all asleep

She often tells me of her past,
Of places long before ,
So she stays on book case shelf,
Not locked behind a door.
My grandson says they all are bad,
They are his greatest fear,
Perhaps he's heard their murmurings,
At night when they are near.
I hope he keeps their stories
And writes them down someday,
For Anna Belle is restless
And wants the light of day.
But a soldier boy must carry on,
Play games, play guns, play war,
But always be the look out man,
For what's behind the door.

Just a Wednesday Afternoon Thought

He often said the blinking light
Would keep him safe, on track
And often I have heard him say,
Will always bring him back.

A good-bye hug now lasts awhile,
For he is now a man.
His world has grown past the light
And opened bigger plan.

Still, coon and gators hold a part,
The swamp is in his soul,
He left and is among the world
But he is in control.

Long ago I placed him in
The hands of loving Lord
And seeing in him happiness
Brings me a great reward.

I've grown old, but get around,
Though eyes have grown dim,
I pray the blinking light remains
And always calls to him.

The Pasture Shack

It was just a wee and little shack,
   Not built by any code.
It sat beneath the pasture trees
   And way back from the road.

So many times I walked the path
   That led me to the yard.
I picked my way thru limb and brush,
   Sidestepped the window shards.

On many walks I took grandkids,
   To let them look around;
We'd find a shell, a rusty pot
   That lay upon the ground.

The buckets, boards told stories,
   Some short and some were long;
We'd touch the boards along the wall,
   Some rotten, some still strong.

We sat upon the rusty springs
   That once held those asleep.
They'd look around for little things,
   Some treasure they could keep.

Each time they came I studied them,
   Hoped stories that we told,

Would stay with them as they have me
Now that I'm growing old.

I prayed that as the years all passed,
Those moments would not die
And all the tried and olden things
Be seen thru Mamaw's eyes.

For now the shack no longer stands,
A place time has forgot,
But I remember walking here
Telling stories on this spot.

I pray in years when they are old
They do what I once done....
Tell stories in a run down shack
To daughter and to son.

I pray they always see much more
Than rusty bed or chair.
I hope they squint their eyes and see
What they saw when we were there.

Gulf Hammock

The Barrel

I saw it sitting in the back
Of my daughter's shed,
Amazing how the stories filtered thru my head.
It's just a metal barrel
With a curved and rounded bead,
It tightly held the cover on and held the years of feed.
A friend of mine had moved away
And left it there with me
And so begins the barrel tale, brought forth from memory.
I look beyond the scratches now,
 the dents and all the stain,
To the time I measured out the horses daily grain.
It was back in sixty-eight,
The first bag entered in,
Joe was young and almost broke, I was young and thin.
All the mornings, afternoons,
The horses heard me call,
The barrel held each scoop of feed that went into their stall.
So many horses ate the feed,
Some stayed, some went, some came,
But when I see the barrel now, it brings back just one name.
It brings back all the memories,
So many have a part,
But now the barrel brings to mind the one that owned my heart.
He took me thru the miles of youth,
My kids would learn to ride,

My barns would change, but feed went in the barrel right inside.
It happened on a cool eve,
Joe crossed the rainbow shore
And as I knelt beside him there I could lift the lid no more.
So it got handed down to kids,
It's dented, has a crack,
But after almost twenty years, I think I'll get it back.
There's a horse out in my pasture;
I could use the barrel now,
But I don't know if time is right, if heart would yet allow.
Next year it will be fifty years,
Since first bag emptied in,
Joe has long since left my side and I'm not young and thin.
The barrel shows a little age,
Scratches, dents and dings,
There's fifty years of summer time, of winters and of springs.
But out there in my barn I've saved,
Joe's bridle, bit and comb,
And now I think it's way past time, Joe's barrel's coming home.

A Sister's Thoughts

We stopped that night,
aggravated with traffic,
Aggravated with each other.
We knew dark roads and pine woods
Made it hard for two pair of old eyes.
Sleep came in pieces,
For I listened to traffic going west
And I wanted to be heading west too.
The light of the camp bathroom
Glowed thru the camper windows.
I listened to mosquitoes, to snoring
And to traffic going west.
At three I wandered to the restroom,
Washed my face and dressed.
An all night radio played my granddaughter's
favorite song
And I wondered,
Could I leave my children and theirs
To be close to her.
I sat at the picnic table, searching the sky
For the faintest glimmer of morning.
This is a child's Christmas I thought, packages ready
to open
While parents slept.
I made enough noise in the camper
To wake those a dozen spaces away.
Soon the way west was before us.

It seemed forever,
Spent on breakfast and interstates,
 listening to the thumps beneath us
And reading mile markers.
At last there were road signs I remembered
And her drive lay just ahead.
We drove thru wagging dog after dog
And she was there.
There were hugs and "How are ya?"
There were smiles and laughter,
There were days of remembering.
But time sped by as it does,
When hearts are light and times are good.
There were no cameras
For they bring the reality of leaving,
Of capturing time in a photo.
Then the morning came,
The one I knew was coming,
The one I dreaded before we left our road
The week before.
For days I had marked my memory
With her laughter, her voice,
For those would have to keep me company,
For months, perhaps a year.
Husband shook hands with brother-in-law
And I hugged, thinking how lucky he was to have her.
It was time and I wanted to postpone it,
For a moment, for two, for a day.
I looked away, burning her place into my mind,
For memories are all we will have.
But it was time and I held her,
Words were choked and cut off in grief.
I held her, for a hug is to last a long while.
We slowly drove away,

Leaving her in her world and taking me to mine.
I looked back once, but could not see,
For eyes could not focus through tears.
I looked back once
And knew the hug was not long enough;
There was more to talk about,
More memories to make,
More laughter to share.
And I thought of our long ago childhood,
When I was not so fond of her
And now I look back once......
For twice would break my heart.

Looking Back

I took a little memory trip, down a tree lined hammock drive,
Past all the cedars, pencil thin, that barely were alive
When I placed them in the ground thirty years before.
Now I think as stiff as I am, I could plant no more.
The trees still shade the grassy yard, their branches neat and trim,
I still must lean to walk beneath the mossy covered limb.
I'm sure the breezes whisper still, though muffled, not so clear
And I wonder if the others know, a mother's soul passed here.
I hear the voice of playing kids, each grandchild owns my heart;
I guess I never thought of it, that they would have a part
In bringing kids into the world, while I, so far away
Would hold unto the pictures sent and keep them on display.
Though now I walk it's halls and rooms, it's not the house I miss,
It's child's squeals, it's memories, a grandchild's nightly kiss.
I stop a moment, look around and reach for husband's hand.
He built the house, fenced the fields, cleared the plot of land.
But memories are not just mine, to own like costly gem.
He is a part of all I am and he is part of them.
He's happy here and life is good, that house has long been sold.
My grandkids grow and have their own, while he and I grow old.
Sometimes at night I will recall and strain to hear the sound,
Of children's voices, tables set, when they were all around.
I know their on a journey, making memories their own,
That they were lent by loving God, a priceless, ageless loan.
Now trees are not so nearly large as those we left behind

And size of house and property has certainly declined.
The family's grown much larger now, still hard to say good-by,
We started this, just me and Bud, it's still just Bud and I.

Gulf Hammock

Our Hands

We were kids when we fell in love,
You handsome, not so bold.
You stole my heart that summer night,
When I was fifteen summer's old.
So many roads we've both been down,
But always as a pair;
When I look at you now I don't see the years
And you don't see silvery hair.
At night when I pray, I am thinking
And I always think of the worst.
I can hear your breathing, so deep in sleep
And I pray the Lord takes me first.
For another hand will never fit mine,
When the time comes that we must part,
There's been only one that has entered my life,
There's been only one in my heart.
So if I go first I'll walk slowly,
All heaven will understand,
We'll enter the rest that is promised,
As always me holding your hand.

Fifty Four and Counting

Just seventeen and twenty-one,
More life ahead than past.
I still can hear my father say,
That this will never last.
I'm sure he thought there was no chance,
No wisdom and no wealth,
And so we ventured on with life,
Just us, our youth and health.
His calloused hands would clear the way,
Midst orange groves and the pine.
We built the fences, built the home
With his hand holding mine.
We had such blessings every year,
But soon a son had died,
He never knew just what to do
So held me as I cried.
We watched as children grew and left,
Faced all that life demands,
Twenty, thirty, fifty years
We still were holding hands.
We go to doctors more it seems,
And don't do what we're told;
He lies and tells me I look good
Though wrinkled now and old.
Now Parkinson's comes into view,
A road we'll undertake,
The hand I've held these many years

Has started now to shake.
The doctors say a mild case,
That's what it now appears,
He might slow down a little bit,
Could be this way for years.
Through good times, sad times, we have grown
And now it's 54,
I hold his hand and think how blessed,
Only God can love him more.
The Lord's been good to both of us,
We've walked life side by side;
When he was but a young girl's groom
And I, his child bride.

POW, POW, POW

He wants to be a soldier, courageous, brave and bold.
I watch him play with army men, he's barely four years old.
His birthday now is looming near, his "I wants," same as then,
When asked what birthday gift he needs, it's always soldier men.
Forever yelling, "Pow, Pow, Pow," at imaginary foe,
His aim gets better every day, as I watch him shoot and grow.
I play the army games he loves, though knees give out and creak,
For I am nearing seventy-one and he is four next week.
I know I'll never see the day, for me and Papa both,
Will not be here to see him take, whatever soldier's oath.
But for as long as I am here, I'll play his army game,
I'll watch him grow, leave me behind, get better at his aim.
But in the midst of playing war, before he gets to old,
Before his uniforms are real, I'll steal a kiss and hold
The little man who yells, "Pow, Pow" and always wants to play,
I'll hold him just a bit more tight, before I'm called away.

7/7/18

He Is Only Lent

Who can know the little man that holds my heart,
Of each word that he says that I hold dear?
This little man that holds the world I know,
While the space between us grows with every year.
But who shall say when I must let him go,
Though he is leaning more to others now.
I hope within my spirit I will know
And be able to let go of him somehow.
But he is seven and I'm forty more,
His friends now take the space I used to fill.
I watch him play and always as before
I pray and place him in God's loving will.
But in my selfishness I will repent,
For I hear God whisper, "He is only lent."

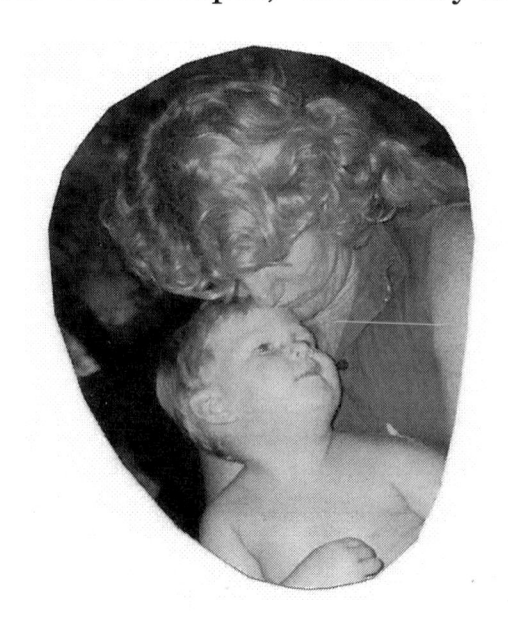

Wasted Time

I remember the kind of day it was, first clouds, then pelting rain
the kind of day most people hate and their favorite day to complain.
But me, I love to hear the rain pound against roof and eave.
It's the kind of day I love to write, when thoughts are dreams believed.
But at five o'clock the screen door creaked and my tired, soaked husband came in.
I knew distraction soon would come so I cleared away paper and pen.
"Been writing hugh?" he finally asked, in a playful, scoffing way.
Then popping the top to his beer he asked, "What else have you done today?"
"Your serious," I then replied, he smiled with nodding head.
"I'd like to know how you can sit and write for hours," he said.
"Well, first I took a little trip down a soggy, southron lane,
Cannons boomed, horses squealed and slipped in driving rain.
There amid the battlefield, a young boy, silent lay.
I knelt and said a prayer for him in his bloodied jacket of gray."
My husband smiled and drank his beer, then to my unbelief he said,
"At least the men you dream about all seem to end up dead.
If that's the only thing you've done and it took eight hours to do,
I hope if I should die tonight I come back to life as you."
He took another swallow of beer and teasingly kissed my face.
"I wish I had all the time that you so freely waste.
Where else has that crazy mind taken you today?

With all the paper scattered here, you spent some time away."
I smiled and started reading him the lines I'd written down,
About a hazy memory, of a home place I had found.
And as I read of home and child, I knew he couldn't see,
It wasn't home I visited, but the child I used to be.
He shuffled feet and tapped my pen, quite bored I could tell.
Then finally said, "If your wasting time, write something you can sell."
I smiled back while thinking of the soldier boy in gray.
He lay there gentle on my mind as I put my things away.
That night while fixing dinner, my thoughts raced far ahead.
Why stupid me, I'd have more fun if my soldiers weren't all dead.
So tomorrow I'll write of a general, quite handsome, dressed in gray.
I smiled at the thought of my husband's shock, when he asks what I've done today.

No Option

Under early dawn stars you left,
Without good byes,
Fading into an eternity
That will never be marked
By your presence.
There is no marker
To kneel and talk over,
No plot to reminisce,
No stone to say
You have ever lived.
Your only flowers were roses,
Strewn among ashes
As they found their way to the river.
Do you know of the pain you've left,
Unable for me to work out?
Why did you take that quiet place?
Was it because I, so headstrong
Never needed it before?
Should I have listened to your wishes,
No funeral, no crying over the dead?
I think not
For my soul cries every day.
Your son is now dying,
And with whom shall we bury him?
I've tried to pick up the gauntlet,
But the burden is to heavy
And you've left me
With no place to go.

On A Visit To His Daughter's Home

He choose the small room,
The room with bureaus
Papered in frame memories,
Stern appearances
Captured on the cloudy film
Of yesterdays memoirs.
He choose the small bed,
The bed that faced
The beveled mirror of his past.
Near to parents,
Near to the grandparents
That touched life with tenderness,
Nearer still to the portrait
That held a part of him.
Yet each morning
As I made his bed,
I could tell she had been moved.
Her picture had not leaned so
The night before.
Like the portrait he held
Their union had withered,
Died a one way death,
Forever making him captive
To the small room.
To the small bed,
To a place he speaks of dreams
And what might have been.

Perhaps A Memory

Sunlight dances over treetops
Spilling onto the ground
In shadowy dapples
Of Lookout Mountain.
I tell my grandson of
Gray suited men
That fought and died here
Five lifetimes ago.
Together we close our eyes
And in the memory of another time
We pretend to hear
The feet that marched before us.
He lets me ramble
About battles and cannons,
About red rivers that cradled the dead
And lent coolness to the living.
I wonder if the ghosts that whisper to me
Will one day reveal themselves to him
And call him back to the place
Mamaw talked of soldiers and things,
Where sunlight dappled the ground
And we stopped to remember.

The Porch Railing

I sit here today, not feeling much good,
Have the 'Woe is me.' on my mind.
Just sittin' here getting' older each day,
and weary and tired of the grind.
Christmas is closing and sure getting' near,
As I watch the lights on the tree,
My mind wanders down the dusty old road,
I follow the child that is me.
How many years did that child have faith
And knew that a pony'd be there,
How many years did I kneel at my bed
And say the same Christmas prayer?
I knew in the morning' a pony'd be tied
To the porch railin' there just for me,
How many years was there no pony there,
Was it ten, was it five, was it three?
I lost track of the time as it grew into years,
That child, now a momma and wife,
Made sure that my kids got every horse
A child could wish for in life.
Strange how life makes a full circle
As I sit in my old parlor chair,
Staring at newly lit Christmas tree lights,
But remembering back through the years.

When You Called Me Lynn

The house is quiet
And the smell of turkey and sweet potatoes
Follow me from room to room.
I count back the Thanksgivings
To the time you were here.
I need to hear 'Lynn' again,
For only you, Dad and Bonnie
Ever called me that
And now everyone is so far away.
Today there will be laughter,
From children and grandchildren.
Today we will eat from your china
In a house you never knew.
I wonder how many holidays
Will pass before I stop looking for you.
As I walk through scented rooms,
I listen for your voice
And am thankful I remember
The sounds of those days,
When we laughed in the kitchen
And you called me Lynn.

The Flood

I saw a picture of a house, was just a little shack,
Instead of seeing what was there, my memories flooded back.
Now who can know what sparks the mind and sends it on a roll,
Remembering buried times of life that we lived long ago?
I try to keep my memories, clear and neatly filed,
But this old house led me back to days I was a child.
I studied boards that held it up, could barely just survive
And thru the dusty years of time, transported me to five.
The years of youth are quickly spent, we barely are aware,
Of slower walk, weakened eyes, of gray and thinning hair.
So often times I take a walk and fight against the fog,
Till I am just a five year old and have my collie dog.

We once again walk the trails of youth, both she and I.
But I grew up and she grew old, still walking by my side.
I watched my father on that day, the day I saw him weep,
That awful day that cancer choose, to have her put to sleep.

I keep her picture by my desk, her collar in my drawer,
So many dogs I've had since then, but none I have loved more.
A furry horse a neighbor bought and told me he was mine,
He often bucked, taught me to ride, when I had just turned nine.

The magic of a child and horse, is freedom in your hand,
For those who never held the rein will never understand.
I snipped a piece of his old tail, I still have to this day
And cried into his graying mane, the day we moved away.
The years passed very quickly, had a husband and a child,
When he informed me he had bought a stud colt, young and wild.
A horse that he had never seen, was never touched before,
Just told me he was stocking red, would never tell me more.
At first sight I said, "Let's go home, he's wild as a coot."
I prayed he'd break his skinny neck while he was in the chute.
But husband just proceeded on, colt now frothy foam,
Roped and tied his very first and he was coming home.
I watched as he began to grow, fill body out and mind,
The boney colt had grown up and wild had turned to kind.
We must have rode a million miles, on and off the grids,
He aged with me, but then went on to raise all of our kids.
Thirty-four had slowed him down, the horse I loved, adored,
Would now lay down the final time and rise for me no more.

Again I snipped a strand of tail, still red with wisps of gray,
It's in a drawer with other things I've saved onto this day.
And now it's time for me to think of something that I dread,
I can not touch the scissors, though I know what lies ahead.

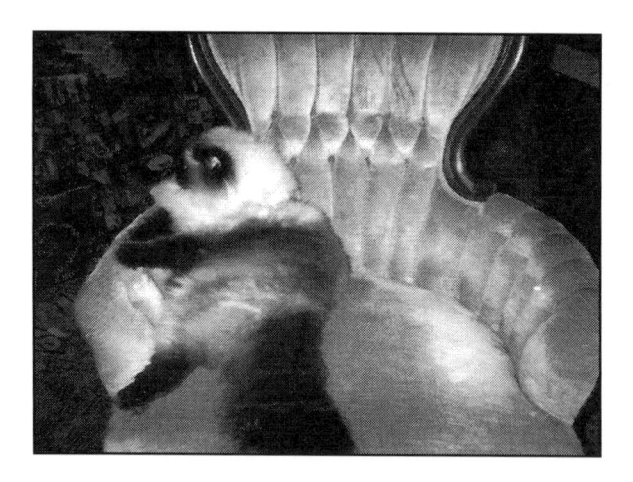

He lays there sleeping on my lap, for more than twenty years.
I hear him purr, I watch him fail and curse the day that nears.
Soon another memory of life that went before
Will be beside two strands of tail and collar in my drawer.
A picture of an old home place, just a little shack,
Instead of seeing what was there, my memories flooded back.

Epilogue

The house now is to quiet, my Mosby has passed on,
I stop to check his water bowl, forgetting he is gone.
I take another memory, like a trinket on display,
Take my tears and broken heart and put it all away.
I take it all and box it up with those that went before
And make a promise to myself, there won't be anymore.
For twelve years he's been close to me, this dog now by my chair,
I wonder when the time will come to clip a bit of hair.

My little shack is filling up with memories of my past,
But as the years are passing me, they are leaving much to fast.
I lean and pet a furry head and scratch a furry ear,
It's part of life to say good-by and love them while their here.
It does not matter how I age, I'll always have a shack,
A place to go to gather thoughts, when memories all flood back.

Sad Thoughts Nearing Christmas

I think of all my Christmas pasts,
When presents were all hid,
My wants were larger than their pay,
But I was just a kid.
And as the tree lights flicker now,
It always makes me sad,
How much I miss who went before,
My mother and my dad.
How fast I wanted to be old,
To be out on my own,
To say good-by to parents then,
To wave good by to home.
The Lord's been good these many years
And memories make me glad
But always this time of the year
I miss my mom and dad.
It's they who made the special time
That came 'round once a year,
But I was young and did not know
The memories I'd hear.
The echoes of my Christmas pasts,
Call me without a doubt,
And leave me looking to the years
Before I was without
A mother's good nite kiss at night
And covers pulled to snug,

A father's warning, "Stay in bed,"
Said after every hug.
And now I sit, have music on,
tunes from long ago,
I watch excited great grandkids,
And think of days they do not know.
But this year will be different,
My sister's on her way
And nieces, nephews, young and old
Will have her Christmas day.
Their memories will circle them,
Though memories aren't the same,
Both they and sister will recall
That special day she came.
And I will hug her neck and cry,
Thankful of the time we had,
A sister that I barely see,
Part me, part her, part mom and dad.

A Poem for My Sister

My sister up and told me that I was getting old,
I wasn't writing near as much, that brains had turned to mold.
And so I started thinking, I've traded in my flair,
My handsome southern soldiers were now my rocking chair.
So give me just a moment to regain my solitude,
Let me dream a little bit till I can change the mood.
You ready now for me to start, to write a poem and spin?
Let's all go back a hundred years. You ready? Let's begin...........

He rode a midnight stallion into my yard that morn,
His jacket frayed and bullet stained, his britches, ragged, worn.
He slipped down from the saddle and I was horrified;
His bullet wounds were caked with mud, I hurried to his side.
He leaned on me and tried to walk, his breath was slow and weak.
I looked away to try and hide the blush upon my cheek.
I brought him to the parlor, was all he would allow,
I washed his wounds, said a prayer and wiped his fevered brow.
All through the night I heard the sounds of rockets, cannonade
And hoped they would not find him on a senseless yankee raid.
But that was all so long ago, the south was in her prime.
The years have passed and not so well and I've lost track of time.
So still the roads are now-a-day, our cemeteries filled
With all our gallant, southern men, the best, the yankees killed.
Yet hope is all that we have left, the rest is burned away.
Our chimneys stand, still straight and tall, they're witness to the fray.

Twas in the eve a stranger came and knocked upon my door,
A dusty frock, a feathered cap, left over from the war.
I looked beyond to see his mount and I was drawn aback,
The stallion stood there quietly, his color, midnight black.
So straight he stood and took my hand, gave me a soft embrace.
I turned away to try and hide the blush upon my face.
But that was then and this is now, the blush is still the same.
I have no guilt, I don't look back and never carry blame.
The fire smoldered on the hearth, it's smoke rose to the sky,
Our clothes lay piled on the bed and I, no longer shy.

Well there I stop this little trip, lest tingling on my skin
Will show that I have been away, my husband just walked in.

Sleepless in Florida

How often when I fight for sleep and know the morning's near,
I often walk the sparse filled rooms and look for pioneers.
I linger in and out of sleep, oft times I feel a poke.
I let my mind pass through the years, till I can smell the smoke.
I can't tell if its creaks or sighs, or boards about to break,
In slumber that has not yet come, I lay there half awake.
Oft times the whispers are not clear, I'm sure 'they' made the choice,
But till sleep comes and conquers thoughts, I strain to hear a voice.
I walk through rooms I've never known, where strangers once had dined,
Where oil lamps and candles glow, familiar in my mind.
I feel the heat of fireplace, the scrapes of boot on floor,
I fight against oncoming sleep and strain to see much more.
I look through wavy panes of glass, into another time,
Always fighting through the years, to make their memories mine.
I smell the heat of summer day and jasmine night time wisp,
I see their piney rooter hog, just trying to exist.
I hear a door then slowly creak and close, it's near almost,
As if another night will wait, for me to meet my ghost.
I fight against the fairy dust and try my best to keep,
My thoughts on those that went before, I fight against my sleep.
And in the morn I'll sit and write, of all the years between,
Of pioneers and families and what I almost seen.
And as I lay again in bed, I'll try again to slip,

Back tween the years that separate and find another trip.
It seems as if it's every morn, I'm tired as before,
But I can't wait to go to bed and find another door.
I almost touch the wavy glass and memories will creep
Into my mind and in the mist, I fight against my sleep.
I lay there hours wide awake and toss and turn in bed,
And tell myself there's time to sleep, when I am finally dead.
Until then I'll try all the doors and hope I get inside,
To tell the tales of pioneers, before 'they' finally died.

Acknowledgements

I want to thank everyone that allowed me to use their pictures in this book. The cover photo was taken by Andrea Sadock. This old Cracker house sits in Micanopy, Florida. I'm sure many people have stopped and listened for the whispers of the hearty pioneers that lived and left a piece of themselves for us to wonder about. As Florida gets paved over, I pray we will always have places left that speak of our past and touch our hearts.

Linda Lee

Made in the USA
Columbia, SC
02 September 2019